Pathways to Independence

DISCOVERING INDEPENDENCE NATIONAL HISTORICAL PARK

By Shirley Milgrim

Illustrated by Richard Fish

The Chatham Press, Inc.   Riverside, Connecticut

ACKNOWLEDGMENTS

We would like to express our appreciation to Martin I.
Yoelson, Supervisory Interpretive Specialist of Independence
National Historical Park, for his guidance in research, his
chapter-by-chapter critiques and his sustaining encourage-
ment in the two years required to complete *Pathways to
Independence*. We also thank Frank Barnes, Penelope H.
Batcheler, John D. R. Platt and John Milley for their expert
and friendly suggestions, and the staff members of Independence National Historical Park for their cooperation without which this book would not have been possible.

— SHIRLEY MILGRIM
RICHARD FISH

Title page illustration: Syng inkstand,
Assembly Room of Independence Hall.

Text copyright © 1974 by Shirley Milgrim

Illustrations copyright © 1974 by Richard Fish

Library of Congress Catalog Card Number: 73-89767

SBN 85699-101-5 (hardcover edition)
SBN 85699-102-3 (paperbound edition)

Printed in the United States of America

Pathways
to
Independence

CONTENTS

Foreword 7

Map 10

1   Gloria Dei (Old Swedes') Church 13

2   Friends' Meeting House 17

3   Christ Church and Cemetery 25

4   Library Hall 31

5   St. Joseph's Church 35

6   Independence Hall 41

7   Mikveh Israel Cemetery 55

8   Franklin Court 59

9   Carpenters' Hall and Court 69

10   Deshler-Morris House 75

11   City Tavern 79

12   Graff House 85

13   Kosciuszko National Memorial 89

14   Todd House 93

15   Bishop White House 99

16   Congress Hall 105

17   Old City Hall (Supreme Court Building) 109

18   Mother Bethel Church 113

19   First Bank of the United States 117

20   Second Bank of the United States 121

21   Philadelphia Exchange 125

Walnut Street garden.

FOREWORD

THE four-block area bounded by Walnut, Sixth, Chestnut and Second Streets in Philadelphia, Pennsylvania, encompasses one of the most important concentrations of historic buildings and sites in the United States and comprises the nucleus of Independence National Historical Park, which was established by an act of Congress in 1948 "for the purpose of preserving for the benefit of the American people . . . certain historical structures and properties in Philadelphia . . . associated with the American Revolution and the founding and growth of the United States."

The Park is among the largest, most complex and ambitious ventures in the preservation of historic landmarks ever undertaken in this country. Since its founding, historians, architects, archaeologists, curators and interpretive planners have meticulously restored, renovated and re-furnished more than a score of buildings important to the period from 1774 to 1835. While most of the funds have been provided by the National Park Service, many private groups as well as the City of Philadelphia have joined directly or indirectly in the project. The city owns those properties within Independence Square and has preserved them since 1818. The Carpenters' Company owns Carpenters' Hall, and the American Philosophical Society owns Philosophical Hall and Library Hall, while the Army, Navy and Marine museums were developed in cooperation with private military associations. Independence Mall north of Independence Square was created by the State of Pennsylvania to complement the federal government's restoration of the area to the south and east.

Pathways to Independence tells the story of the people and the events that wove the fabric of American independence. Each chapter is designed to stand on its own and be read by the visitor to any particular building or site. The chapters themselves are arranged in chronological order, and thus the book as a whole traces the growth of Philadelphia from the Swedes who preceded William Penn, through the early nineteenth century. Of necessity to give the complete story, some historic places which are not a part of Independence National Historical Park have been included. These are: Friends' Meeting House, Free Quaker Meeting House, St. Joseph's Church, St. Mary's Church, and Mother Bethel Church.

The dedicated men and women who have joined together to apply their expertise to the creation of Independence National Historical Park, as well as those who have worked to preserve other historic sites nearby, deserve the heartfelt gratitude of the American people. More than merely restoring paint, mortar, brick and stone of long-neglected buildings, they have unveiled in Philadelphia a shrine to the rights of men for the benefit and inspiration of millions of people from all parts of the world.

Dock Creek Bridge.

God grant that not only the love of Liberty
but a thorough knowledge of the Rights of Man
may pervade all the Nations of the Earth,
so that a Philosopher may set his foot anywhere
on its surface and say, "This is my country."

— BENJAMIN FRANKLIN
December 4, 1789

INDEPENDENCE
National Historical
Park

Sites keyed to chapter number

1. Gloria Dei (Old Swedes') Church
2. Friends' Meeting House*
2a. Free Quaker Meeting House
3. Christ Church
3a. Christ Church Cemetery
4. Library Hall
4a. American Philosophical Society
5. St. Joseph's Church*
5a. St. Mary's Church*
6. Independence Hall
7. Mikveh Israel Cemetery
8. Franklin Court
9. Carpenters' Hall
9a. New Hall
9b. Pemberton House
10. Deshler-Morris House *(not shown)*
11. City Tavern
12. Graff House
13. Thaddeus Kosciuszko National Memorial
14. Todd House
15. Bishop White House
16. Congress Hall
17. Old City Hall
18. Mother Bethel Church*
19. First Bank of the United States
20. Second Bank of the United States
21. Philadelphia Exchange
22. Independence Mall
23. Visitor Center

Sites not included in Independence National Historical Park

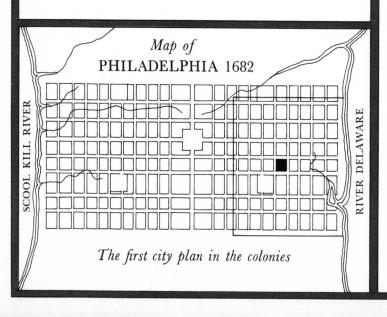

Map of
PHILADELPHIA 1682

SCOOL KILL RIVER

RIVER DELAWARE

The first city plan in the colonies

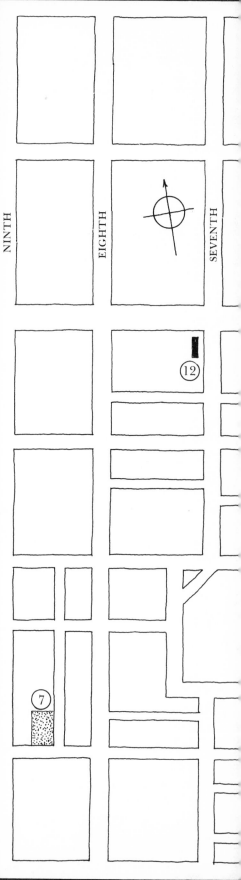

NINTH

EIGHTH

SEVENTH

⑫

⑦

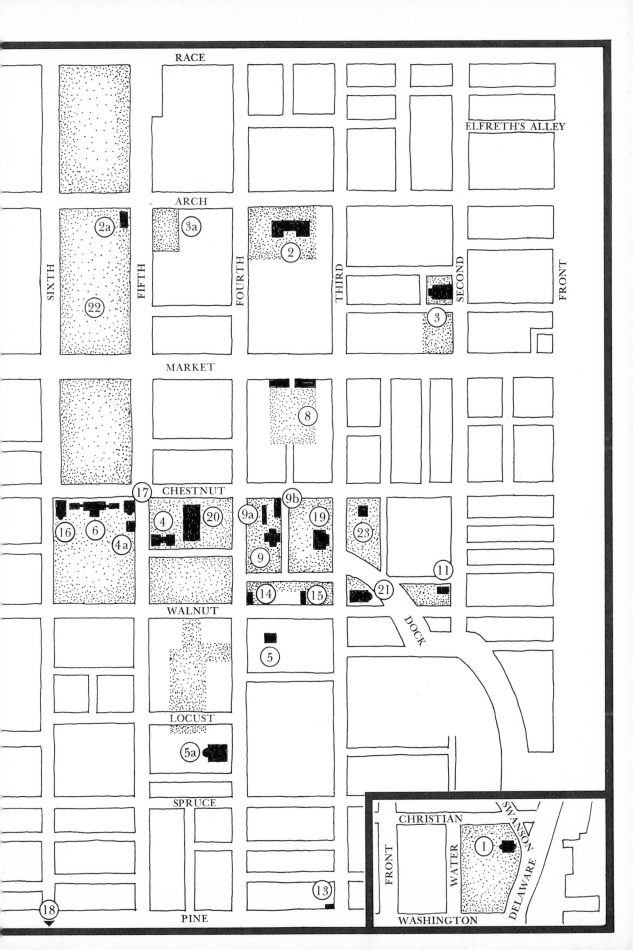

Gloria Dei (Old Swedes') Church and graveyard.

GLORIA DEI (OLD SWEDES') CHURCH

1

Christian Street and Delaware Avenue. Erected in 1700 on the site of a 1699 blockhouse once used by the Swedish Lutherans as a mission of the Church of Sweden, Gloria Dei is the oldest church building in Pennsylvania.

ALMOST forty years before William Penn arrived to establish what would become the Province of Pennsylvania, a party of Swedish colonists sponsored by Queen Christiana settled near the mouth of the Delaware River. The Swedes were big and powerful and skillful with the axe. In a short time they had raised a community of solid houses for themselves and under the leadership of their governor, Johan Printz, built a church, a simple fort and an official governor's residence on an island in the Delaware called Tinicum.

In 1669 a number of Swedes, who for many years had heard the local Indians refer to "Wicaco," north of Tinicum, where the earth was fertile and the forests abounded in game, rowed up the river in small boats to locate this "pleasant place." They found it on the western shore of the Delaware, just below the area where Philadelphia would be plotted in 1681. Here a new community was built with a log blockhouse to be used for worship as well as for defense. The men cleared fields, planted tobacco, corn and other grain, and on nearby Cobbs Creek helped their Governor construct a mill that ground "fine and course flour and was going early and late." The Swedish women spun and wove cloth, and with the gifts of the forests around them made tea and dye from the sassafras tree, brewed beer and brandy from persimmons and crushed bayberries to make candles and cure toothaches.

The Swedes and the Leni-Lenape Indians of the area dealt fairly with each other and the settlements along the Delaware passed many peaceful years. Even when the Dutch conquered the Swedish colonies in 1655 and the English took possession from the Dutch in 1664, the Swedes adjusted amicably to their new governors and went quietly about their affairs. They were an honest, God-fearing people, imbued with the spirit of civil liberty; qualities that would be declared ideal a century later by a struggling new American nation.

William Penn's arrival in 1682 with his Quaker followers did not make malcontents of the Swedes. The Quaker leader's dream was also their dream; here was a land where equal opportunity for all would prevail. They willingly accepted Penn's "Holy Experiment" in the New World and volunteered to help him with one of his earliest tasks; taking a census of their community. Penn, who had feared animosity from the established settlers, wrote a friend in England that the 907 Swedes had declared the day of his arrival "The best day they ever saw!" And one of Penn's lieutenants wrote home, "They [the Swedes] will build you a house without any other instrument but a hatchet. With this one tool they will cut down a tree, cut it into pieces in less time than two other men could do it with a saw; with this instrument and a few wedges of wood they make planks and whatever you wish . . . ."

In 1691 King Charles XI of Sweden sent a missionary of the Swedish Church, the learned and talented Reverend Doctor Andreas Rudman, to Wicaco as religious leader for the little community south of Philadelphia. No sooner did he see the crumbling old Swedish blockhouse where two missionaries had already served than he moved to build a new church. Rudman wrote to Sweden, "The population is very thin and scattered along the river shore so that some have sixteen miles to walk or ride to go to church. Never the less they very regularly attend divine services on Sunday." Surely such faithful people deserved a proper house of worship!

Where would the new church be located? Communities at Swede's Crossing and Tinicum, as well as Wicaco, all wanted the church nearby. Rudman solved the dilemma by placing strips of paper in a hat and picking one. Wicaco was chosen and all three settlements donated money to the building fund. The widow and daughter of Sven Shute, a Swedish military hero in America who had been awarded eight hundred acres near the river by Queen Christina in the colony's earliest years, contributed the ground for the church.

The dedication of Gloria Dei took place in 1700. William Penn attended and presented the church with a "Breeches Bible" (so called because the overly modest translators of Genesis 3:7 had Adam and Eve put on breeches instead of fig leaves to hide their nakedness). Charles Calvert, the governor of what is now Delaware and Maryland, marveled at the simple beauty and dignity of Gloria Dei, while Andreas Rudman wrote home that, "The English, who now govern this province and are beyond measure richer than we, wonder at what we have done.

Gloria Dei was a rectangular, red brick structure; its interior consisted of a main hall with a small balcony, the whole dominated by a pulpit at one end. The church's few ornaments included a bell, a baptismal font and a wood carving of two cherubs mounted on an open Bible reading in painted letters, "The people who wander in darkness have seen a great light," and "Glory to God in the highest!" The ornaments had been brought from Gothenberg in 1642 by Governor Johan Printz and were installed at Gloria Dei in 1700.

Reverend Doctor Rudman encouraged his parishioners to apply for English "naturalization" papers, the simple requirement being that they take an oath of allegiance to the new masters of the province. The minister led the way. Earliest Pennsylvania court records show Andreas Rudman's papers dated 1701 to be the first application for naturalization in the province. Rudman died two years later and was laid to rest in front of Gloria Dei's chancel. The tranquil churchyard did not claim its first coffin until 1708.

Toward the middle of the eighteenth century a new pastor, John Dylander, was sent to Gloria Dei. At the time, the German Lutheran population of Philadephia had neither church nor minister, and they asked Dylander to preach to them when he was free from other duties. Dylander, a witty and generous man, was soon sermonizing at Gloria Dei three times every Sunday; at nine in the morning in German, at ten in Swedish and after dinner in English. The English version attracted so many people that the overflow stood outside the doors and windows straining to hear. After the Germans built a church of their own in Germantown, the energetic Dylander preached there once a month, as he also did at Lancaster. During some weeks the pastor delivered sixteen sermons.

John Dylander died of yellow fever while propped up in bed performing a marriage ceremony. Over the protests of his wife who wanted him to conserve his strength, he had insisted that he end his work on earth this way. The pastor's funeral at Gloria Dei drew such a crushing throng that "hysterical ladies lost pieces of their skirts" while squeezing along the blocked aisles, and dignitaries made themselves ridiculous by climbing through windows to reach their pews.

Maps of Philadelphia from this period show the city's boundaries to be the Delaware River on the east, the Schuylkill River on the west, Vine Street to the north and South Street to the south. Penn had called the land along the Delaware south from Pine Street to Old Swedes' Church "Society Hill" after the Free Society of Traders, a group chartered by the Proprietor to develop commerce in the area. Under the English, Wicaco was renamed Southwark and became an independent borough of Philadelphia.

As the Revolutionary War threatened, the last missionary to be sent to Gloria Dei from Sweden arrived, Reverend Doctor Nickolas Collin. The intellectual Doctor Collin quickly affiliated himself with several of Philadelphia's many learned societies. He became an authority on colonial Swedes and· wrote home proudly of his Swedish parishioners who were well absorbed in the political life of Philadelphia.

Collin cheered the men of his parish as they enlisted in the army to fight for independence. In 1777 he stood by helplessly as the occupying British tore down for firewood those shops and houses in Southwark vacated by the fighting Swedes. He supervised the removal of the church organ pipes, whose brass metal would be used by the Continental Army, and when the war ceased he saw the bodies of friends killed in the conflict laid to rest in Old Swedes' graveyard. During the last quarter of the eighteenth century Gloria Dei retained its tranquil setting while a tide of postwar industry brought a lumber yard, a factory for staining paper and making ink, and the United States Navy Yard to the area.

In 1789 the Swedish Archbishop permitted his clergymen to end their missionary work in America and return to Sweden. But Nickolas Collin, the last of the Swedish pastors, chose to stay and serve as pastor of all the Swedish churches in Pennsylvania. He had adopted the English language at Gloria Dei and had begun to employ Episcopal assistants. Collin died in 1831 and fifteen years later Gloria Dei was received into the Episcopal Church.

Old Swedes' Church has served its parishioners continuously and well through the years. To this day it inspires such loyalty in its members that many of the faithful, though they no longer live in Southwark, still "very regularly attend divine services on Sunday," as Andreas Rudman said nearly three hundred years ago.

Baptismal font, Gloria Dei.

FRIENDS' MEETING HOUSE

2

Arch Street between Third and Fourth Streets. Erected in 1804 on land given the Quakers by William Penn in 1693 to be used for a burial place, the Meeting House is still in constant use. It houses an exhibition on early Quaker life.

I N the fall of 1682, before winter's breath could freeze and block the Delaware, a small sailing ship followed the gulls through the river's uncharted shoals to New Castle. The *Welcome*, though not the first vessel to bring a weary band of English immigrants to the New World, could still claim distinction, for it carried William Penn, leader of the Quakers and "True and absolute Proprietary," to his province.

To Penn the landing seemed a miracle. His ship had been pummeled continuously by gales during the eight-week crossing of the Atlantic, and thirty of the one hundred Friends aboard had died of the plague and been dropped into the waves. Penn had just begun to believe that he, like Moses, might lead his people to a promised land but never live to set foot on it when the amber woods and tangled banks of his destination came into view and his spirits soared.

The truth of the old adage that good often results from bad situations struck Penn. Only three years before, Britain's Parliament had attempted to crush all dissenters from the Church of England, particularly country Quakers who, though required by law to attend the state church, stubbornly insisted on the right to hold their own public meetings for worship. The viciousness of the newly elected governing body of Britain even caused

King Charles II discomfort, for the handsome and charming William Penn, leader of the Religious Society of Friends, was the son of Admiral Penn and a court favorite. The easy-going monarch had no stomach for ordering William imprisoned.

England had wrested a vast territory west of the Delaware River from the Dutch in 1664. The royal family, with wilderness to spare but short on money, had offered it for sale with no success. Now Penn made a suggestion to his King that Charles settle a sixteen-hundred pound debt to the Penn family by making him "Proprietary by Royal Charter" of the territory between New York and Maryland west of the Delaware River. Penn would develop a refuge there for all persecuted people; a "Holy Experiment" in political and religious freedom. A perfect solution to his Quaker problem, King Charles agreed.

To launch a colony was a mammoth undertaking even for a man such as William Penn, who had studied at Oxford, been schooled in the law and was endowed with intelligence and the ability to persuade. But Penn, at the peak of his mental and physical powers, resolved to succeed through careful planning. Never was a colony so meticulously thought out before-hand. Penn drafted a constitution, his first "Frame of Government," and sent newly appointed officials ahead to America to guide the development of a "Great Towne" on the Delaware. Realizing that both settlers and investors would be needed, he first recruited colonists from the persecuted minorities found in the English and German countrysides, most of whom were artisans and farmers. Then he wooed wealthy Quaker investors who shrewdly saw in Penn the perfect mix of visionary and practical man.

The territory had boundless resources, Penn told the investors. Situated in the middle of the colonial seaboard, its capital, which he called Phila-delphia or "The City of Brotherly Love," would become a natural center for commerce. He would sell country land outside Philadelphia in blocks of no less than five thousand acres, and would require that for every five acres cleared, one must remain forested. Then, for every five hundred acres a man owned in the outlying areas, Penn would award him ten city acres as a bonus. Investors could immigrate or not (two-thirds remained in England as absentee landowners). They could hold their property or sell it, or they could lease small plots to people of modest means who wanted to live in the capital and ply their trades there. Penn also gave hope to refugees with no means at all. Their passage over would be paid if they became indentured servants for two years; an idea seized upon by about one-half of the settlers who arrived in Pennsylvania during the first six years.

What did it mean to be a member of the Religious Society of Friends, or "Quakers" as the followers of George Fox were called by those who taunted them? A Friend was a "friend to all mankind" who styled himself after the apostles; a simple person enlightened directly by the spirit of God.

Friends' Meeting House, Fourth and Arch Streets.

He found no need for a government-supported priesthood cut off from everyday life, or for formal programs of worship and music. A Friend's inspiration came from ordinary men and women, neighbors perhaps, who regularly came together in an unadorned room to settle down in silent waiting. When moved to rise during a meeting and share an inspirational thought, he would do so. He refused to pay taxes or support the Church of England, and he strictly observed the Biblical command to "live at peace with all men." He would not serve in an army, make munitions, or sell goods for war use. Nor would he pay military taxes.

When arrested for disobeying the law and brought into court, a Friend stood in silence during the proceedings. The Bible said to "swear not at all," and thus he could not serve as witness or juror. His cause was further weakened when he declined to doff his hat out of respect for a judge or other person of authority because the Bible taught that "all men are equal in the sight of God." Thus Friends were despised and ridiculed by the "Churchmen" of England. As their lives grew increasingly hard, they boarded ships at Bristol and sailed to Philadelphia; many even arrived before William Penn.

Once on dry land, Penn was not a man who wasted time looking back. Having gone through the formality of showing his deeds of possession to the Swedes and Dutch at New Castle, he proceeded to a settlement called Upland, which he re-named Chester. Here he arranged for the election of an assembly and a council to govern the province and in late winter of 1682 or early spring of 1683, these gentlemen voted upon and adopted Penn's "Great Law." Finally Penn arrived by barge at the juncture of the Delaware River and Dock Creek where the deputies he had sent ahead in 1681 had laid out streets grid-fashion on the west bank of the river, according to a city plan first drawn by Thomas Holme. Already an inn and a number of houses in various stages of completion gave the town an appearance of order.

The Quaker artisans whom Penn now saw at work erecting the new buildings had on their arrival a year or more earlier, hollowed out caves in the high river bank to shelter their own families and then offered their skills for hire. Tradesmen from London, gentry from Ireland and Wales, a sprinkling of former navy officers and the wealthy merchants who arrived in short order, all clamored for their services. A few of these workmen now greeted William Penn. Those who had never seen him could not believe that the broad-shouldered, tall and athletic looking, thirty-nine-year-old gentleman wearing a blue sash could be their Proprietor.

Until Penn's arrival, Friends had been gathering for worship in private homes. But now they put up a "boarded meeting house" known as Bank Meeting House, overlooking the river on Front Street north of Arch. Bakers, brewers, smiths, carpenters, brickmakers and merchants donated the sixty pounds required to build it. Those who could not give money contributed labor or materials. The structure was made to look as unlike a "steeple-house" as possible. For thirteen years it would accommodate not only the regular meetings of local Quakers but also the Yearly Meeting of Friends from Pennsylvania, New Jersey and Delaware. In addition, the Provincial Assembly would meet there.

Penn applied Quaker principles to the colony's relationships with the Leni-Lenape Indians. He lived with them for a short time, formed a high opinion of their integrity and purchased land from them under several treaties whose terms were always honored. In 1683 he wrote: "We [Penn and the Leni-Lenape chiefs] have agreed that in all differences between us, six of each side shall end the matter. Do not abuse them, but let them have justice and you win them." The Friends kept this faith with the Indians and enjoyed peace for over fifty years.

Then, in 1684, Penn was commanded to appear in court in England. He expected the visit to be short and assigned wealthy associates to govern in his absence and to protect his rights as Proprietor. His stay lasted fourteen years, however, and in that time his "loyal" associates forsook Penn's interest to look after their own, as conditions in the colony changed and one problem after another surfaced.

A Scot named George Keith tried to reform the Religious Society of Friends while Penn was away, and in the attempt aroused the working people to resentment of Penn's practice of awarding political power to social leaders. At the same time, the trickle of immigrating Anglicans increased to a stream and the Quakers found themselves in danger of being swallowed up by the very adversaries they thought they had eluded in England. Moreover, these churchmen from Britain were bringing Black slaves to the City of Brotherly Love; a condition abhorrent to most Friends.

On April 18, 1688 at the Monthly Meeting in Germantown, the Quakers delivered the first public pronouncement ever made in America against slavery:

> There is a saying that we shall do to all men . . . as we will be done to ourselves; making no difference of what generation, descent, or color they are. . . . In Europe there are many oppressed for conscience sake; here there are those oppressed which are of black color. . . . Have these Negroes not as much right to fight for their freedom as you have to keep them slaves?

Penn struggled back to his province in 1700 to find Philadelphia's population had leapt to five thousand people; an Anglican (Christ) Church had already risen on Second Street and was serving a congregation of seven hundred. To Penn's dismay, a Church of England Party had gained a political foothold in government with the rallying cry, "Strip Penn of his proprietary rights and return this colony to the Crown!"

The trusted associates Penn had left in authority had become self-seekers who, observers noted, each "prayed with his neighbor on First Days (Sundays) then preyed on him on the other six." Moreover, they had no time for the Proprietor. Appalled by their treachery, Penn tried to take comfort in the fact that at least outside the political arena Quakers displayed extraordinary concern for humanity. Indians were being fairly treated, slavery opposed and penal reforms encouraged. A few years later the Quakers would support widows, shelter orphans and teach them trades, build poorhouses where self-respect for the residents was a major consideration, and speak out loudly against war.

Also comforting to Penn was the fact that Quakers still flocked to worship. The Bank Meeting House having decayed rapidly and been removed, a Great Meeting House, fifty feet square, had been erected at Market and Second Streets.

England summoned Penn once again to settle serious personal financial problems. In 1701, before leaving America for the last time, he faced his detractors in Pennsylvania's government. Gone was his old charm. With iron determination he forced the adoption of his revised Frame of Government which he called his Charter of Privileges and which was to become the Pennsylvania "Constitution." It remained in force until 1776 and in a sense foreshadowed the United States Constitution by providing for religious freedom and complete separation of church and state.

The first half of the eighteenth century found England with many enemies and the port of Philadelphia open to blockades or attacks by pirates and other belligerents. In addition, Pennsylvania's western frontier was undefended against the encroaching French because Quaker provincial leaders upheld their principles of nonviolence and would not authorize a military force.

A frantic, non-Quaker faction of government pointed out to the Friends that they no longer comprised the majority of the population; two-thirds of the people recognized that the survival of the colony depended upon arming it. In all good conscience, the Quakers must stop seeking public office if their religious principles adversely affected the safety of the majority. The Friends agreed that they had no other choice than to step down from government, but they let it be known that they would never remain silent on issues.

In 1776, when the decision was made by the Continental Congress meeting in Philadelphia to proclaim independence from England, the Quakers declared themselves neutral. And a year later when cannon boomed in nearby Germantown, they calmly sent a testimony against the Revolution to both General George Washington and British General Howe. At the same time, a group numbering about one hundred Friends announced they were Tories while some four hundred others joined the American army or accepted positions in the revolutionary government. Both groups were disowned by the parent body.

Upon termination of the war, the four hundred "Fighting Quakers" built their own Free Quaker Meeting House at Fifth and Arch Streets, about four blocks away from the Great Meeting House, through public subscription. Among the first to donate to the project were Benjamin Franklin and George Washington, who understood what torment their decision to take up arms had caused these Friends.

In 1805 the Great Meeting House at Market and Second, already over one hundred years old, was sold and the proceeds used to build a new meeting house on Arch Street between Third and Fourth Streets, where the Quakers had buried their dead since 1693. A sturdy brick structure was erected with committee rooms and a large hall with a gallery capable of seating sixteen hundred participants in Quarterly and Yearly Meetings. The Meeting House was unadorned and furnished with simple benches.

The Friends' Meeting House at Fourth and Arch Streets has been in constant use to this day. On its original benches now sit in silent meditation the descendants of William Penn's highly principled and industrious seventeenth-century followers. Though not as plain in dress or language as their ancestors of the Colonial period, the Quakers still speak their minds on issues and continue to fill the role that fell to the Friends as the colonies united; the role of the nation's conscience.

The pulpit of Christ Church.

CHRIST CHURCH AND CEMETERY 3

Second Street north of Market. Constructed between 1727 and 1744, Christ Church is the oldest Anglican church in Philadelphia. Two signers of the Declaration of Independence are interred in the churchyard and five others in Christ Church Cemetery at Fifth and Arch streets.

WILLIAM Penn received his patent for land in America in 1681, and the Bishop of London, fearing that Anglicans might be excluded from the Quaker "Utopia," insisted that King Charles II insert a provision in the patent that, "wheresoever twenty inhabitants request a minister of the Church of England to reside among them, they shall be allowed to do so . . ."

Penn, however, had no intention of excluding "Churchmen." His promotional pamphlet, printed in four languages, invited all who prized religious freedom, liberal government and land on easy terms to come to Pennsylvania. A mix of different nationalities and religions that never before had been tolerated in a British colony quickly populated his province and from the first year made it thrive. So glowing were the reports carried back to the counting houses of London that Anglicans put aside their distaste for people who worshipped differently and joined the fortune hunt on the banks of the Delaware.

In 1695 Philadelphia's Anglicans built the first Christ Church, a small wooden building on Second Street north of Market, not far from Bank Meeting House. Quakers who passed by, comfortable in their numbers, could not have dreamed at the time that their former tormentors, wealthier, better educated and more aggressive than most other colonists, would one day displace them in government and dominate the political and social scene of Philadelphia. By 1700, however, seven hundred Anglicans complained that their church could not seat them all and they began to solicit donations for a larger structure.

Work finally began on the foundations of the new Christ Church in 1727, at first on a rather bizarre note. As the laborers dug into the mud of the churchyard, skulls and caskets of previously interred church members came to light. A flustered vestry ordered the widow of a former sexton to be paid "for picking up and burying the bones" in Christ Church Burying Ground at Fifth and Arch Streets. Seventeen years later the church emerged "happily finished" and inspired a visitor to write, ". . . . Christ Church has by far the most venerable appearance of any building in the city and the whole architecture would not disgrace one of the finest streets in West Minster."

To some citizens Christ Church looked like its parishioners: sober and elegant. It was a rectangular brick structure with a white steeple of Baroque ornamentation. The interior furnishings displayed the skill of Philadelphia's cabinetmakers, who would later have a claim to fame for their Chippendale-style furniture. A large, Palladian window looked east to the Delaware; fluted Doric columns supported a gallery; and from the ceiling hung a British-made, twenty-four-branched chandelier. The library contained close to a thousand theological folios and volumes, some of which were printed in the fifteenth century and presented as gifts of Queen Anne. Started in the earliest days of Christ Church by missionary Thomas Bray, the collection now found a new home in this building.

Doctor John Kearsley, one of a three-man committee (all members of Christ Church) involved in the building of the State House, designed Christ Church and ordered a ring of eight bells for it from England. These arrived in the hold of the ship *Myrtilla*, whose captain, Richard Budden, declined payment and forever after was welcomed to Philadelphia's harbor by the pealing of the Christ Church bells.

By the middle of the eighteenth century, Philadelphia's waterfront bustled with shops, offices, taverns, tanneries, stables, malting houses and lumber yards. Viewing it from aboard a ship in the Delaware, the city resembled London, but with one glaring difference. According to a visitor, "Philadelphia, with its ninety houses of public worship, boasts only two or three steeples to strike one's attention." The following year a two-hundred-foot spire was added to Christ Church, dwarfing the surrounding buildings.

At this time Baptists, Jews, Presbyterians, Quakers, Catholics and Episcopalians all lived peaceably side by side in William Penn's City of Brotherly Love. High intellectual and moral standards prevailed. A university had been established and schools dotted the area, several of which welcomed girls as well as boys. The mistress of a school for Black children led her pupils to Christ Church Wednesdays and Fridays to be catechized. Deborah Franklin wrote to her husband Benjamin, then in London, "I went to hear the Negro children . . . at church. There were seventeen that answered very prettily indeed and five or six that were too little, but all behaved very decently. . . . It gave me a great deal of pleasure and I shall send Othello to the school."

Affluent members of Christ Church began to build houses on Third Street between Chestnut and Spruce. They found it increasingly difficult to struggle from these city "outskirts" to the church six blocks away. Although there were wooden foot-walks, winter snow drifted deep on the rutted streets and in other seasons mud and pooled water blocked them. Thus they pressed for a new house of worship closer to their homes but still under the aegis of Christ Church. St. Peter's Church at Third and Pine Streets resulted. Reverend Jacob Duché, who at the time held the title of Assistant Minister of Christ Church, performed double duty as St. Peter's clergyman.

When Britain and France went to war over their New World territories, the colonies reached out to each other for self-protection. Philadelphia, halfway on the rude road connecting the southern settlements and New England, became a communication center. And, because its members held high political offices, Christ Church became the most influential religious body within that center.

The French and Indian War ended favorably for the British, and the colonies looked forward to a more peaceful life without French soldiers attacking their western frontiers. But to their dismay, England now began to assert a new, severe authority in America. Unreasonable taxes and trade restrictions angered the colonists. Britain squeezed harder and Philadelphians flocked to church to hear sermons on the need for more local autonomy and an Englishman's inherited liberties. Complaints became the battle cry, "No taxation without representation." When Paul Revere brought word to Philadelphia that the British had blockaded Boston harbor, the muffled bells of Christ Church tolled a "solemn peal at intervals from morning to night."

In September of 1774, representatives to the First Continental Congress of colonies to the north and south hastened to Philadelphia to decide what to do about this latest outrage. While in town, George Washington from Virginia and John Adams from Massachusetts attended services at Christ Church, where it was said that Whig members of the congregation were demanding Tory members be barred from church. The energetic John Adams later climbed up the dark, winding staircase to the steeple to get a full view of this major American city, never dreaming it would be occupied by the British Army within three years.

Each Sunday Christ Church's minister, the Reverend Mr. Jacob Duché, spoke out ardently from his pulpit on such subjects as "The Present Situation of American Affairs" and "The Duty of Standing Fast in our Spiritual and Temporal Liberties." His sermons were printed and widely distributed, and the Continental Congress made him their chaplain. The Congress prayed as a body at Christ Church in 1775 and 1776, and listened with rapt attention to the sermons. Such flattering attention inflated Duché's ego while tales circulated that he now sat long hours every day having his hair curled and powdered.

At first Duché reveled in his role as a patriot. But when British General Howe began his advance toward Philadelphia in 1777, Duché seemed to lose his zeal for the cause of independence. British troops occupied Philadelphia in the fall of 1777 and imprisoned Jacob Duché (along with Reverend Coombs, also of Christ Church) for one night. Duché decided then and there that only reckless fools would take up arms against the most powerful empire in the world. The French would never come to the aid of the colonies and without their assistance, all would be lost.

Congress fled to York, Pennsylvania, leaving its chaplain behind. Duché felt obliged to write his opinions to General Washington, now struggling to keep his army together at Valley Forge. The minister added as a final thrust to his ill-timed letter that the men who served under the General were rabble and, of all of Washington's officers, "very few are there you can ask to sit at your table." Washington did not respond.

The British army settled into comfortable Philadelphia homes for the winter of 1777-78. They put so many houses to the torch that the view from the top of Christ Church "was a prospect of fires." Yet they fought few skirmishes. During a thunder storm in the spring of 1778, lightning struck Christ Church steeple and melted the metal crown atop it. The townspeople whispered that this was a sign King George would soon lose his own crown, and shortly thereafter the British paraded out of Philadelphia for good. In their vanguard marched men, women and children still faithful to the King. And with them went the Reverend Mr. Jacob Duché, ex-Chaplain of the Continental Congress, who once prayed for the deliverance of "our American states."

Until the Revolution a good part of the salaries for Anglican clergymen had come from England. Then payment ceased and in all of the Province of Pennsylvania only the young but highly respected Reverend Mr. William White of Christ Church remained at his post. Congress nominated him to replace Duché as their chaplain and Reverend Mr. White, even though it seemed then that the revolutionaries could not succeed, unhesitatingly swore his allegiance to the American cause.

In 1787, the remnant of the Protestant Episcopal Church of Pennsylvania convened at Christ Church and appointed the Reverend Mr. White to sail to London to be consecrated Bishop. On his return, a golden Bishop's miter replaced the crown above Christ Church. Two years later the most important convention ever held by the Episcopal Church in America met there and adopted a constitution, canons and a prayer book, making the church independent of British ecclesiastical politics just as the nation had become independent of the British in secular politics.

When Philadelphia became the capital of the United States in 1790, "The Nation's Church" set aside a pew for presidential use. George Washington attended services at Christ Church only once in a great while, but Martha Washington and her grandchildren regularly arrived in the presidential coach drawn by dazzling white horses.

Today the graves of seven signers of the Declaration of Independence (including Benjamin Franklin) can be found in the Christ Church grave-yard and its cemetery. The church, continuously in use since colonial days, still retains its original character. Its steeple no longer dominates the city skyline and commercial buildings have crowded around it, yet it is still possible to perceive the description of Christ Church that appeared in the *Pennsylvania Gazette* in January of 1772, ". . . in point of elegance it surpasses everything of its kind in America."

Front facade, Library Hall.

LIBRARY HALL

4

Northeast Corner, Fifth and Library Streets. The present building was erected in 1959 by the American Philosophical Society. The Fifth Street facade and the western portion of the structure represent the original Library Hall which was constructed in 1789-1790.

IN 1731 Benjamin Franklin gathered together some friends to found the Library Company of Philadelphia with a modest collection of books shelved in a rented room of a house on Jones's Alley, "back of the house in which Mr. Hornor has his iron mongery store." Destined to be the "mother of all subscription libraries in North America," Franklin modeled it after the first library started in England in 1684; but with one improvement. Franklin's association permitted subscribers not only to read the books but also to take them home for a reasonable amount of time.

Philadelphians, already praised for their industriousness and respectability, discovered the pleasures of reading. They saw the pastime as one diversion Friend and Churchman alike could smile upon. Reading, everyone agreed, would remove "grosser relaxations [such as gambling, dancing or theater-going], promote a person's health, enlarge his mind and prolong his life while . . . teaching him to enjoy it."

In the next few years Philadelphians began to send for books from England in the same way that they ordered marble from Italy and wine from Madeira. They donated single volumes and whole collections to the Library Company. Needing more space, the Library moved to the second floor of the west wing of the new State House, later known as Independence Hall, in 1740.

Soon other libraries sprang up. In 1769, at the invitation of Benjamin Franklin, the Union Company, the Amicable Library and the Association Library became one with the Library Company, raising the number of subscribers to six hundred. A busy librarian opened the door six days a week at one PM and turned the heavy iron key in the lock at sunset. In addition to other duties, he patiently answered the questions of such visitors as the Reverend Mr. Jacob Duché who climbed the stairs out of curiosity and reported to a friend, "You would be astonished at the general taste for books which prevails among all orders and ranks of people in this city. The librarian assured me that for one person of distinction and fortune there were twenty tradesmen that frequented this library."

Again needing more room and a location somewhat removed from the noise of the State House area, the Library Company agreed to become the first tenant of Carpenters' Hall, just finished a block-and-a-half away. The Carpenters' Company fitted out the upper floor of their building to the needs of the Library. The books were transferred in 1774 in time to offer the First Continental Congress, meeting in the ground floor of Carpenters' Hall, use of the volumes.

During the Revolution the Library Company found itself located above a hospital for disabled soldiers on the ground floor of Carpenters' Hall and a storage center for army supplies in the cellar. But other than extraordinary wear on books borrowed by the British during the occupation of Philadelphia in 1777-78, the Library did not suffer during the war years.

By 1789 Philadelphia's population was nearing 70,000, a serious housing shortage had developed, and prices were increasing rapidly. As a result, Carpenter's Company raised the Library Company's rent to a point where the aged but still practical Benjamin Franklin advised the Library to erect a building of its own. The directors advertised in the newspapers for architectural plans "as elegant as the unavoidable frugality of the place would admit" and offered one share in the company as a reward for the design chosen. Some notable gentlemen entered the contest, including Thomas Jefferson, but Quaker physician William Thornton won the prize.

Edinburgh educated, Doctor Thornton had recently arrived in Philadelphia from his home in the West Indies in search of a bride and a lucrative medical practice. He was just discovering how paltry were the fees paid Philadelphia physicians when the Library Company's advertisement caught his eye. Architecture had always interested him. So with little more preparation than a quick study of Abraham Swan's *Collection of Designs in Architecture,* he submitted plans and elevations to the directors; and won the contest. The self-confident young man deserted medicine for good that day and began a career in architecture that reached its peak a few years later when he designed the Capitol Building at Washington, D.C.

The raising of Library Hall on a piece of Fifth Street property that had once been part of the Norris family's garden became a community project. Dozens of workmen accepted shares in the Library Company as pay for their labor. Dedicated by Benjamin Franklin to "The Philadelphia Youth," the structure was completed in 1790. With its Georgian-style facade, a niche over the front door where, after his death, Franklin's statue would be installed, and its balustrade and pedestals for seventeen urns, Library Hall drew from *Pennsylvania Gazette* editors the typically Philadelphian praise word, "elegant."

That same year the fledgling United States government, which had convened for a brief period in New York City, returned to the scene of the Declaration of Independence and made Philadelphia the temporary capital of the nation. Library Company's directors immediately invited all government officials to "use the books in the Library . . . as if they were members of the Company," a privilege the Library had extended to members of the Continental Congress and the Constitutional Convention in previous years. It was a gesture which presaged the establishment of the Library of Congress in Washington, D.C. ten years later.

The first floor of Library Hall consisted of two rooms, one of which held five thousand books and the other ten thousand. Both rooms were ornamented with paintings, maps on rollers, busts of George Washington and Benjamin Franklin and a statue of Diana. In the subscribers' room the highest shelves were reached from a light gallery which ran across the front. On the second floor could be found a room with a table and Windsor chairs where once a month the directors feasted on a "collation of oysters and fish house punch." In another chamber the librarian demonstrated scientific machines on Saturday mornings from ten to twelve.

Library Hall provoked some criticism during the early part of the nineteenth century. One spit-curled woman wondered why Philadelphia Library directors resisted "amorous love novels." Another complained of the haze of cigar smoke that hung over the gallery in the late afternoons. A gentleman opposed to the late hours of opening declared, "Men may trifle with books in the afternoon, but they must be studied in the morning." He then pointed out, "Indeed, no one . . . in the Philadelphia Library ever dreams of any higher effort of mind than to gaze with half-shut eyes at Hogarth's prints or maps on the wall, to read a magazine or revue, to discuss the . . . last *Gazette* or quietly sink on the shoulder of the armchair and enjoy a long vision of the Muses."

A visiting Englishman recommended the Philadelphia Library to his friends as the "coolest room in the city for a nap," and praised the powers of a half-dozen students there whose concentration was interrupted only "by profound snores, convulsive twitching and the grinding of the teeth and other symptoms of the most studious slumber."

For fifty-five years the Library Company served the community in its

Fifth Street building. By 1856 Philadelphia's population had spread west from the Delaware halfway to the Schuylkill River and the directors realized their location was no longer central. They moved out in 1880 and the old hall was sold and torn down four years later. In 1959 the American Philosophical Society erected a replica of Library Hall and added a new wing, but the Fifth Street facade and western portion of the building represent the original structure. The dimensions of the new building were adapted to the space requirements of the Society's library, which now occupies it.

ST. JOSEPH'S CHURCH

5

Willing's Alley near Fourth Street. The first Roman Catholic Church in Pennsylvania was established here in 1733. Mass has been celebrated continuously on this site for more than 240 years. The present structure was built in 1839.

EARLY in the eighteenth century, Jesuit missionary Joseph Greaton rode his horse north on the Indian trails from Maryland to conduct Mass for a handful of Catholics in the Province of Pennsylvania. He visited the villages of Frankford and Germantown outside of Philadelphia, then gathered the few Catholics living in the city to worship in a private home. Father Greaton went quietly about his work with an eye on the local authorities. Roman Catholic Masses had been outlawed throughout the British Empire in 1688, and the law had been strictly enforced in Britain's American possessions until 1707 when Queen Anne ruled that Masses could be said, but only in a chapel which was part of a "living house."

Greaton had heard that outside of Maryland, a colony originally established as a haven for Roman Catholics, not a single Catholic Church existed in the English colonies in America. But, he thought, now the time had come to try to build a public Roman Catholic house of worship. Philadelphia might well be the city to permit it, since Quakers who dominated the provincial government rejected restrictions imposed upon them by England in favor of their own liberal Charter of Privileges.

Father Greaton settled in Philadelphia in 1729 and, four years later, acquired land at the edge of town. The site sat well back from Walnut

Entrance to St. Joseph's Church from Willing's Alley.

Street between Third and Fourth on a rise overlooking apple orchards and meadows as well as Clarke's Hall, the grandest residence in the city, and the neighboring Quaker Almshouse and City Almshouse.

Wondering how soon he would feel the hand of the law on his shoulder, Father Greaton supervised the construction of an inconspicuous building to be called St. Joseph's. It had neither tower nor steeple to call attention to its religious purpose and resembled a house on the outside, but on the very day the church was consecrated, Pennsylvania's Lieutenant Governor Patrick Gordon voiced his concern at a session of the Council. It had been brought to his attention, he said, "that Mass is openly celebrated by a Popish Priest in violation of the Act of Parliament extending to all the King's dominions!" What action did the Council propose to take? The Council decided, with all due respect to their monarch across the sea, that they would uphold Pennsylvania's Charter of Privileges which protected every man's right to practice publicly the religion of his choice.

Jubilantly, Father Greaton went to work enlarging St. Joseph's membership. From thirty-seven persons it slowly doubled, with German immigrants outnumbering the Irish. The priest petitioned his superiors abroad for one English-speaking assistant and at least two German assistants, a difficult order to fill in England where Jesuit priests still hid in the countryside and funds to support missionaries to America could not be raised.

But help came from a titled convert to Catholicism who sponsored a missionary, Father Henry Neale, in 1741. Upon his arrival in Pennsylvania, Neale reported by letter to his patron:

> I must of necessity keep a horse in order to assist poor people up and down ye country some twenty miles some sixty, some farther off. Little money can be expected . . . ye country Catholics . . . are most of them servants or poor tradesmen more in need often times of charity themselves than capable of assisting others.

Another priest joined Father Neale in Philadelphia and two young German Jesuits settled in Conestoga. Aging Father Greaton was recalled to Maryland and Father Robert Harding replaced him. Harding, a well-educated and gregarious man, found himself in a bustling city of shops, markets, schools, churches, public buildings, paved streets and rows of brick houses, a few being built as far west as St. Joseph's. A gentleman by the name of Willing had purchased the property behind the church for a new home and cut an alley through the block, giving St. Joseph's a second access.

The new priest involved himself in the cultural institutions and the social problems of Philadelphia, which had become a refuge for the world's persecuted. As the city's population rose, he found himself serving a new and exotic congregation which included Seneca Indians converted to Catholicism by the French (now at war with the English on Pennsylvania's frontier for dominance of North America) and Acadians of French descent who had been turned out of their homes in Nova Scotia by the British army and shipped south to the colonies.

The day that three sloops loaded with Acadian exiles anchored in the Delaware, fearful Philadelphia officials sent Quaker philanthropist Anthony Benezet abroad to see if the new arrivals were dangerous. Benezet found no agents of the French military on the vessels; only pitiful men, women and children stripped of their homes and possessions because they would not swear allegiance to England, and now suffering from smallpox, hunger, cold and fear.

The Acadians needed a refuge and Benezet pleaded their case to the Assembly. It granted permission for the "French neutrals" to stay in Philadelphia and allotted public funds for their relief. The refugees swiftly found their way to St. Joseph's Church where Father Harding offered whatever religious comfort he could for their sad situation.

St. Mary's churchyard.

The arrival of this large group of French Catholics prompted nasty demonstrations against Philadelphia's Catholic population, for the very day the Acadians dropped anchor, news came that British General Braddock had been defeated by the French. Even worse, there had been a savage attack by the French and Indians on Pennsylvania settlers at Lancaster. An angry mob, accusing all Catholics of being enemies of the people, gathered in Philadelphia

> . . . in great numbers with an intention of demolishing the Mass house belonging to the Roman Catholics. Wherein they were . . . encouraged by people of higher rank. But the peaceable Quakers insisting that the Catholics as well as Christians of other denominations were settled upon the faith of the Constitution or William Penn's Charter of Privileges and that the government were bound to protect them so long at least as they remained inoffensive and paid dutiful regard to the establishment . . . The Magistrates . . . with a good deal of difficulty prevailed with the mob to desist.

To Father Harding's distress, however, suspicion continued for several years. "Papists" could not hold office, and rigorous oaths were made obligatory to keep Catholics out of the militia. Their houses were searched for arms and the government was kept informed of their numbers. In and around Philadelphia in 1757 lived nearly four hundred English, Irish, French and German Catholics, with 1,365 Catholics in Pennsylvania as a whole.

St. Joseph's, now too small to serve its parish, was razed to make way for a larger building. The new structure, so plain that it had "more the appearance of a stable than of a church," possessed only one ornament in its dimly lit, whitewashed interior — a painting of the Madonna by Benjamin West which hung over the altar. The new church building's chief enhancement seemed to be Father Harding himself. The priest had been accepted in the community as a "decent, well-bred gentleman, much esteemed by all denominations . . . for his prudence, moderation, attachment to British liberty and unaffected pious labors." Even the snobbish Reverend Duché, Rector of Christ Church, visited Father Harding in his "little Carthusian cell" and described St. Joseph's warmly as "an old Gothic chapel."

In 1763 an adjunct to St. Joseph's Church, named St. Mary's, rose on part of the older church's graveyard on the West Side of Fourth Street above Locust. Father Robert Molyneux and Father Farmer replaced Father Harding as war with England loomed. The sympathies of the Catholic community in revolutionary Philadelphia were as split as were the loyalties of other denominations at the time. While 180 Roman Catholics organized into a regiment to serve Great Britain, about eighty-five percent of the parishioners of St. Joseph's and St. Mary's were patriots.

When Catholic France and Spain became American allies in the Revolution, Philadelphia's Catholics emerged for the first time as an important and influential group. In an effort to cement the Franco-American Alliance, Congress (with only one Catholic member) attended as a body a Requiem Mass at St. Mary's Church on September 18, 1777 held for General Du Coudray, a French officer. Next, on July 4, 1779, at the invitation of M. Girard, the French Minister, the members attended the chanting of the Te Deum in celebration of the anniversary of independence. On May 8, 1780, they were present for a Requiem Mass for Don Juan de Miralles, a Spanish agent. At this time an observer wrote:

> I found there not only Papists, but Presbyterians, Episcopalians, Quakers, etc. The two Chaplains of Congress [one a Presbyterian and the other a Church-man] were amongst the rest. I confess I was pleased to find the minds of people so unfettered with the shackles of bigotry.

Finally, on November 4, 1781, Congress celebrated a Mass of Thanksgiving at St. Mary's for the final defeat of the British at Yorktown by the combined American and French armies.

In the years after the Revolution, St. Mary's Church attracted many prominent parishioners, including Commodore John Barry and refugees from the French Revolution, while people of modest means continued faithful to St. Joseph's. At least one outstanding figure did prefer a pew at old St. Joseph's Church. Joseph Bonaparte, the older brother of Napoleon and a resident of Philadelphia after 1815, frequented the old church with his two children and a huge Newfoundland dog.

St. Joseph's second church building was demolished to make way for a more commodious structure in 1839. The large brick edifice erected at that time still stands today at the end of the courtyard off Willing's Alley. St. Joseph's has been used continuously for worship ever since and is regarded by many Americans as a national shrine to religious freedom.

INDEPENDENCE HALL

6

Chestnut Street between Fifth and Sixth Streets. Constructed as the Pennsylvania State House, the Hall was first occupied in 1735. It provided a meeting place for the provincial and then the state government until 1799. Here the Second Continental Congress convened in May of 1775 and on July 4, 1776 adopted the Declaration of Independence. The Constitutional Convention met here in 1787 to frame the Constitution of the United States.

IN the early years of the eighteenth century a Council, an Assembly of elected representatives and a Supreme Court governed the Province of Pennsylvania. Lacking a suitable meeting hall, these men gathered in private homes of Philadelphia to transact the affairs of the Province.

By 1729, however, William Penn's "Greene Countrie Towne" had grown to a city of nearly 12,000 people and settlements were being established at an ever-increasing distance from the capital. Assemblymen who rode long miles over crude roads to reach Philadelphia complained that many "rude and disorderly persons" caused them to suffer insults and "indecencies" unbecoming to men of their stature. They demanded that the governor grant them permission to quit Philadelphia, that "object of wonder and admiration," and find a place that was "safe and most convenient," where a building worthy of government could be raised.

The Governor agreed that Pennsylvania needed a State House; lesser colonies already had such buildings. But for the sake of the city's merchants who would suffer if the government left, he advised that Philadelphia remain the capital.

A committee consisting of Doctor John Kearsley, Andrew Hamilton and Thomas Lawrence set to work on State House plans and immediately quarreled. The imperious Kearsley, who had designed Christ Church (then in the process of completion), insisted that the structure should serve both as a State House and a market and should be located in the heart of the city on Market Street near the prison. Andrew Hamilton, former Attorney General of Pennsylvania and a noted lawyer who had defended John Peter Zenger during his freedom of the press trial in New York City, had the loftier idea of erecting several buildings that eventually would comprise a government center. He proposed that the State House complex rise on the outskirts of town and be used solely for government functions. The Assembly chose Hamilton's farsighted plan over Kearsley's and appointed the lawyer to supervise construction of the State House, which he vowed would be a "credit to the whole province."

The site Hamilton purchased for the project, which was to absorb him the rest of his life, extended from Chestnut Street to Walnut and from Fifth to Sixth Streets. The old Coach and Horses Inn, a country tavern, stood on the north side of Chestnut Street and the area was characterized by whortleberry bushes, peach trees and cows grazing in open fields.

Hamilton, inspired by the courts of London in which he himself had stood and guided by illustrations from James Gibbs' *Book of Architecture,* sketched a building for a State House larger than any attempted to this time in the colonies. He hired master carpenter Edmund Woolley to carry out his plans. Hindered by inexperienced workmen who demanded more pay than "thirty shillings per square" (one hundred square feet), Woolley nevertheless managed by 1735 to produce an impressive brick edifice, 107 feet long, two stories high, with a gambrel roof and cupola, and with brick arcades extending out to wing buildings. A central hallway twenty-five feet wide and two forty-foot-square rooms comprised the first floor. The east room could be closed for privacy and would serve as the Assembly Room, while the room to the west would house the Pennsylvania Supreme Court and be open to view from the hallway. Upstairs, partitions had not yet been raised.

Even though the walls were not paneled, windows glazed or plaster work completed, in September of 1735 the legislators, eager to move in, insisted on holding their first meeting in the building. The finishing process would continue around them and above their heads for six more years as the room for the Governor's Provincial Council in the southwest corner of the second floor, a Banquet Hall and a Committee Room for the Assembly in the southeast corner were partitioned off.

Completed or not, the proud Mayor of Philadelphia invited four hundred guests to a State House "housewarming" in the fall of 1736. And in the Banquet Hall or Long Room that extended the entire length of the State House, he provided "everything eatable and drinkable and no scarcity of good humor and diversion."

The State House quickly became the showplace of Philadelphia as well as one of the most ambitious projects yet attempted in the colonies. The men who met there in the dead of winter, however, discovered a few faults. The Assembly Room was cold despite the fact that hickory logs crackled in the fireplaces. Representatives seated at small tables a distance from the Speaker and the hearths fought drafts by tucking the long, green baize table covers around their ankles. Across the hall, the open room of the Supreme Court had no fireplace at all and shivering judges frequently called for the doorkeeper to provide them with footstoves.

An echo problem also plagued the legislators during the early days when Andrew Hamilton reigned as Speaker of the House and Benjamin Franklin served as its Clerk. Franklin commented that he found the reverberating discussions "so unentertaining . . . I was reduced to amuse myself with making magic squares or circles or anything to avoid weariness."

Quaker Isaac Norris, who succeeded Andrew Hamilton as Speaker of the House, improved conditions by ordering curtains and covers for the chairs to absorb the echoes. He further enhanced the Assembly Room by purchasing a silver ink stand designed by Philip Syng for the Speaker's table. Then he asked Edmund Woolley to build a new bell tower connected to the south side of the State House.

In 1751 the Assembly authorized Norris to "get us a good bell" to hang in the tower. The bell would call the members to meetings, ring at times of celebration and mourning, and announce public gatherings. On November 1 of that year the Speaker addressed a letter to Robert Charles, London agent for the colony, requesting him to order a bell of "about two thousand pounds weight," and to inscribe in "words well shaped in large letters round it: 'By order of the Assembly of the Province of Pensylvania [sic] for the Statehouse in the City of Philadelphia, 1752' and underneath 'Proclaim Liberty thro' all the Land to all the Inhabitants Thereof — Levit. XXV 10'."

Cast at London's Whitechapel Bell Foundry, the bell arrived on the docks of Philadelphia in August of 1752. Edmund Woolley was in charge of its hanging, but when the bell was tested, it cracked. "Two ingenious workmen," John Stow, a brass-founder in Second Street near the State House, and John Pass volunteered to recast it. The first attempt failed, and it was not until June of 1753, after a second recasting, that the bell we know as the Liberty Bell was finally placed in the tower. The crack seen today did not appear until the first half of the nineteenth century, and the ringing of the bell for Washington's Birthday in 1846 marked the final blow it received from a clapper.

Once their bell hung in the State House tower, the Assembly authorized clocks to be mounted on the east and west gables of the building with a system of connecting rods to strike the hour on a second bell originally ordered from England as a replacement for the first and set on the roof of the State House for that purpose. Not content with these enhancements, in 1753 Isaac Norris saw to the completion of a Committee Room joined to the southeast corner of the Assembly Room. This elegant chamber would also serve as a library for the Assemblymen, offering them a warm and comfortable place in which to relax with books on English law, history and poetry.

A steady stream of visitors strolled up from town to see the public show in the Supreme Court Room of the State House where a procession of judges in white wigs and scarlet robes, "frilled bosoms and bands," entered through the archways and ascended to the bench to try murderers, burglars, counterfeiters and rapists. As if in a theatre, the spectators groaned or applauded when the judges sentenced those convicted to be hanged, whipped, pilloried, branded on the hand, imprisoned or fined according to the severity of their crimes. Increasingly, Philadelphians bragged that their State House was "the greatest ornament in town."

At the same time, however, many politicians resented Norris' costly improvements, calling his expenditures a Quaker device to avoid using the government's money for defense against privateers in the Delaware or the belligerent French and Indians threatening Pennsylvania's western frontier. Even William Penn's grandson, Thomas Penn (not a member of the Society of Friends), was alarmed for the safety of the unprotected colony. He wrote from England, "I think their hospital, steeple, bell, unnecessary library . . . indicate money being directed into projects tolerable to Quaker conscience." An anti-Quaker faction struggled to topple Friends in government from the powerful offices they had held from the early days of Pennsylvania's colonization and angry debates on armed defense raged behind the closed door of the Assembly Room.

By December of 1757, Scotch-Irish and German settlers west of Lancaster had become embittered by the lack of response from the Provincial Assembly to their pleas for militia, a fort or even a few guns to protect themselves from attacks by hostile Indians. A group of these frontiersmen packed the mutilated bodies of one family in a wagon, drove it to the capital and dumped the corpses in front of the entrance on Chestnut Street. A Mrs. Brown wrote that day in her journal, "I went to the State House to see two men and a boy that were brought into town dead, scalped by the Indians. . . . It was the dismallest sight I ever saw."

Four hundred Germans sympathetic to the frontiersmen stormed into the Assembly Room to demand action of the government. Quakers, who no longer comprised a majority in the Province of Pennsylvania, should not represent people who were not bound by their peace principles. Some action must be taken against the French and Indians who now fought Great Britain on American soil for American territories. The Quaker leaders decided at their own Meeting to step down from public office.

Seven years later the Treaty of Paris terminated the French and Indian War and gave almost all of North America east of the Mississippi to England. Some of Pennsylvania's Indian tribes continued to harass settlers trying to convert Indian hunting grounds into farm land. So long as the Indian cause had not been represented at peace negotiations in Paris, Indian hostility could not be expected to cease.

However, good relations with Indians continued in and around Philadelphia as they had ever since William Penn's day. It was a common sight to see entire families file up the stairs of the State House for friendly talks with the Governor in his Council Chamber or for an Indian dance to be performed there as an expression of good will. For many years, Indians who came to the capital to get supplies slept in the wing buildings of the State House where the Library Company occupied one second-floor room and where the Land, Loan and Rolls Offices and the Office of the Register were located. But the Indians' use of fire so near the public records worried authorities and a wooden shed to house them was erected a little beyond the west wing.

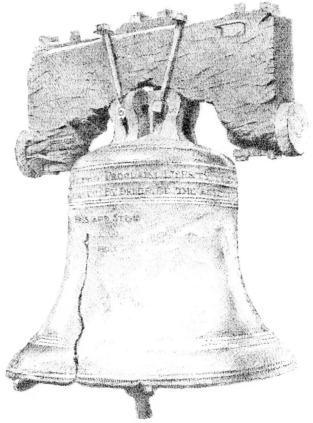

The Liberty Bell.

British officers who served in America during the French and Indian War carried back across the Atlantic Ocean tales of the commercial potential of England's possessions. It was not long before Parliament imposed increasingly oppressive taxes and trade restrictions on the colonies. Outraged Americans with no representation in Parliament drew together to protest such tyranny. Then, in April of 1775, the Massachusetts militia exchanged fire with a troop of British soldiers at Lexington.

Representatives from all the colonies convened in the Assembly Room of the State House in Philadelphia in May of 1775 as a Second Continental Congress. (The first had met eight months earlier in Carpenters' Hall to voice its grievances.) Their immediate action, designed to show Great Britain that the colonies were united and strong in their protest, was to nominate the tall, impressive George Washington of the Viriginia delegation to organize all the Continental forces and to serve as their Commander-in-Chief. Washington, clad in the uniform of a Lieutenant Colonel of the Virginia Militia, "sat but three chairs off and no more from the door of the Library Room," according to John Adams of Massachusetts, and on hearing his name put forward, he "darted into it like a streak of lightning and was seen no more during the deliberations."

Tories from New England to the Carolinas hotly opposed the move toward independence. But a growing number of colonists, stirred by Tom Paine's pamphlet, *Common Sense,* would hear of nothing less. Patriot mobs in Philadelphia ransacked the properties of known Loyalists. Doctor John Kearsley, forty-six years earlier a member of the original State House building committee, but now old and ill, survived an attack on his home only to be dragged to the State House, where "they . . . confined him . . . (and) next morning they took him to the common jail."

The character of the Pennsylvania State House changed overnight from a provincial to a national building. In the Assembly Room, delegates from the colonies attempted to create a new government while a Committee of Safety passed gunpowder and muskets up the stairs to be stockpiled in the East Room of the second floor.

During February the representatives in the State House choked on fumes from two ten-plate stoves and dabbed at their eyes as they wrestled with the question of the colonies' relationship to England. All through that spring, John Adams and his followers called for independence while Robert Morris and other conservatives maintained that the colonies were unprepared militarily and economically. Some delegates suffered such conflicted feelings that even though they spoke out against oppressive England, the thought of separation from it brought tears to their eyes.

Finally on June 7th, Richard Henry Lee of Virginia rose to voice the resolution "that these United Colonies are and of a right ought to be free and independent states. . . ." Four days later a committee was named, consisting of John Adams, Thomas Jefferson, Benjamin Franklin, Robert R.

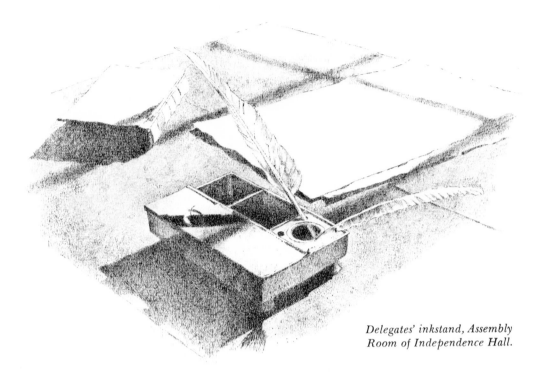

Delegates' inkstand, Assembly Room of Independence Hall.

Livingston and Roger Sherman, to put the declaration on paper in proper legal form. On the insistence of the other committee members, Jefferson agreed to compose the document in his rooms in the Graff House at Seventh and Market Streets.

July 2, 1776, according to John Adams, "will be the most memorable epoch in the history of America . . . celebrated by succeeding generations . . . from one end of this continent to the other from this time forward forevermore. . . ." That day the Congress, after prolonged debate, adopted Lee's resolution. On July 4 it adopted the Declaration of Independence drafted by Thomas Jefferson with revisions. Copies of the document were printed and sent to various individuals, including General Washington, who was instructed to read it to his troops. July 8, a Monday, was designated as the day of proclamation and Colonel John Nixon read the Declaration from a platform in the State House Yard. Following this first public proclamation, the King's coat of arms in the Court Chamber was removed and that night "there were bonfires, ringing bells and other great demonstrations of joy."

Though Tories sputtered and an unknown hand placed a paper in the Assembly Room that warned of a bomb planted in the State House cellar, the Continental Congress would not be shaken from its chosen course against the mightiest empire in the world. The representatives attended religious services to pray for God's help, each well aware that should the war fail, the signing of his name to the Declaration of Independence made him a candidate for hanging. Most of the signers, however, affixed their signatures to the document on August 2, 1776.

In the early fall of 1777 the fighting crept close to Philadelphia. British cannon firing at Washington's troops eight miles away in Germantown rattled the windows of the State House. Recognizing that occupation was imminent, the bells of churches and public buildings were ordered removed from Philadelphia "to some place of safety." They must not be melted down to provide the enemy with cannon and ammunition. The State House bell was taken to Allentown and hidden in the basement of the Zion High German Reformed Church.

John Adams recounted in his diary how, at three o'clock on the morning of September 19, he was "waked . . . and told that the members of Congress were gone . . . some of them a little after midnight, that . . . the enemy had it in their power to be in Philadelphia before morning. . . ." Adams slipped out of the city and hurried to join the delegates from New York and New England in Trenton. Congress would remain together that winter in York, Pennsylvania.

A polished British force under Lord Charles Cornwallis occupied Philadelphia, dragging behind it five hundred Continental captives. Most of the prisoners were herded into the public jail, but forty officers were confined in the upper floor of the State House, the first floor of which became the British Provost Marshall's headquarters. Not for several months did General Washington, camped at Valley Forge, learn that American prisoners suffered unnecessarily cruel treatment. The officers in the State House received no food for six days after they were first jailed. Guards brutalized them, robbed them, withheld their money and letters and deprived them of wood for fires. One man described his ordeal:

> The smoke from the stove below stairs . . . and the badness of the chimneys made breathing intolerable. At the end of December we were to be removed to the new jail where a very malignant disorder raged and we saw six or eight dead bodies taken out to be buried a day.

Washington threatened General William Howe with retaliation against British prisoners if conditions did not change, and Howe made some modest improvements. But in June, when the Redcoats and all their sympathizers paraded out of Philadelphia for good, they left an open pit near the State House filled with dead horses and human corpses. It gave off a nauseating stench and fed countless flies which buzzed in and out of the doors and windows of the building that had once been the government center.

Congress waited only until the odor had abated and the Assembly Room had been cleaned before it moved back into its old quarters. Upstairs the partition between the room in the southeast corner of the building and the Long Room was taken down to create more commodious quarters for the Pennsylvania Assembly. With the exception of a new privy or "necessary"

Independence Hall.

Watchman's box,
Independence Square.

set up in the State House Yard, no further building improvements could be considered. Congress' treasury could not afford even firewood, ink stands or candles for light, should their meetings last into the evenings. It could not pay its members, nor could it meet its obligations to the soldiers in the field with any regularity. The future looked grim.

The indomitable representatives filled with hope, however, at the news that their commissioners in Paris, headed by Benjamin Franklin, had enlisted France as an ally in the war against England, and they offered a fitting reception to the very welcome first French Minister, Conrad Alexander Gérard, when he arrived in Philadelphia. Unaccustomed as the envoy was to government without frills, once Gérard had presented his credentials at the State House, he wrote home to his countrymen that he found the bare brick buildings and the plain, straightforward statesmen admirable.

In the spring of 1781 James Madison of Virginia, a new representative, took a seat at one of the tables in the Assembly Room as the states ratified the Articles of Confederation and Perpetual Union, instituting one government for the thirteen states. Several months later, with the help of the French navy, money from the French military chest and the troops of Count Rochambeau, George Washington and his men surprised Cornwallis at Yorktown and brought about the British surrender. That fall, the twenty-four captured standards that symbolized victory for the Americans and the end of the war were carried to the State House and placed at the feet of the Congress of the Confederation in a moving ceremony.

With the war over, Congress found itself $42,000,000 in debt, and under the Articles of Confederation powerless to levy taxes to raise money. The most pressing debt was owed to the soldiers being mustered out minus several months' back pay. Unlike some soldiers praised by General Washington for having "suffered and bled without a murmur and who with perfect good order . . . returned to their homes without settlement of their accounts or a farthing of money in their pockets," an increasing number of jobless and destitute veterans milled around the State House Yard giving voice to their resentment.

In June of 1783 a group of about three hundred mutinous soldiers stationed in Philadelphia, having identified with the plight of the veterans, demanded that the helpless government produce four months' pay owed them and settle other grievances. With fixed bayonets, they marched to the State House, surrounded it and, "furnished with spirits by the rabble," stayed in position "uttering offensive words and pointing muskets to the windows of Congress" the entire afternoon. The soldiers did no damage and let the Congressmen leave unharmed at three o'clock (their usual hour of adjournment), after which they returned to their barracks. But the demonstration so grossly insulted the authority of government, to say nothing of endangering the peace of the city, that the Congress of the Confederation left the Pennsylvania State House and moved to Princeton, New Jersey.

They would never return to Philadelphia, the representatives said, because in all the four hours they were imprisoned, "not a citizen came to our assistance."

In May of 1787, however, a convention was called to revise the inadequate Articles of Confederation. Presided over by George Washington, the great minds of the new nation once more came together in the Assembly Room of the State House where, instead of making changes in the old "Articles," they formed a new constitution for government. In September the editor of the *Pennsylvania Packet* wrote, "The year 1776 is celebrated for a revolution in favor of liberty. The year 1787 is expected will be celebrated with equal joy for a revolution in favor of government." The Constitution of the United States was signed a few days later.

During the next three years the Pennsylvania State Convention met in the State House and, among other business, ratified the federal Constitution and adopted a Pennsylvania Constitution. The capabilities of men in government at this time amazed Europeans on missions to the United States no less than their appearance. J. P. Brissot de Warville, a Frenchman brought by General Mifflin to observe the General Assembly meeting in the State House, reported, "someone who should fall suddenly from Paris into this Assembly would undoubtedly find it ridiculous. He would scoff at the simplicity of their cloth coats and in some cases the negligence of their toilettes . . . but pointed out to me under one of these plain coats (was) a farmer . . . whose eloquence displays the greatest talent. . . . Everyman who thinks will desire that this simplicity may forever remain and become universal."

The Pennsylvania government continued to occupy the State House when Philadelphia became the temporary capital of the United States in 1790, while Congress Hall and City Hall, the buildings flanking the State House, provided a meeting place for the House of Representatives, the Senate and the United States Supreme Court. In 1800 the federal bodies moved to their permanent home in Washington, D.C. The Pennsylvania government, after doubting that Philadelphia would ever be free of yellow fever epidemics and recognizing a need for a more central seat now that the state had increased its number of western counties, moved to Lancaster in 1799 and to its present seat at Harrisburg in 1812. Though the Court Room was still used by federal and state bodies and the wing buildings were occupied, the other rooms of the State House stood vacant. Slowly the building began to lose its importance and prestige.

In 1802 the Pennsylvania legislature granted artist Charles Willson Peale the use of the second floor and the east room on the first floor of the State House for his museum, which for six years prior to that time had been an attraction at Philosophical Hall.

Peale placed a sign over the entrance to the old building reading, "Museum, Great School of the Nation." He hung the portraits he and his son, Rembrandt Peale, had painted of the great men of the day and put on display his collection of stuffed birds, animals and insects, mineral and fossil specimens, and bizarre machines.

The terms of the artist's agreement with the state legislature made him responsible for maintenance of the State House and Yard. Peale took this charge most seriously, and over the twenty-six years of his occupancy he added more trees to the one hundred elms planted in the yard in 1787, beautified the serpentine paths with pots of flowers and increased the circulation of air by taking down high brick walls and substituting low ones topped by iron palisades. He improved the lawns and set up benches and new gates at Fifth and Sixth Streets. He then installed cages of live animals for the amusement of visitors.

Before the Peale Museum moved away in 1827-28, a celebrated friend of America, the Marquis de Lafayette, who as a youth had served in the War of Independence, arrived from France to see the new country one more time. Nationwide attention focused on Philadelphia's celebration of the aging nobleman's return; the State House was "hung with scarlet and blue draperies studded with stars" for the occasion. For the first time journalists began to refer to the Assembly Room as the Hall of Independence.

Their interest stimulated by Lafayette's visit, Philadelphia's Council hired architect William Strickland to design a new steeple on the belltower very similar to the original which had been taken down in 1781. From this time on, a national awareness of the old State House as a historical shrine slowly developed. John Haviland, also an architect, made the first attempt in 1830 to restore the Assembly Room which over the years had suffered many alterations. The room then became a reception hall for distinguished visitors, including all the presidents from Jackson to Lincoln.

A collection of memorabilia appropriate to the time of the Declaration was started in 1854 with the purchase of one hundred oil portraits by Peale of Colonial, Revolutionary and early Republican personages. These were hung on the walls of the Assembly Room and, along with the Liberty Bell (then called Old Independence Bell) and a wooden statue of George Washington by William Rush, comprised a display opened to the public.

In the middle of the century, a number of Philadelphians could not resist making some practical use of the old State House, national shrine or not. Thus, while bodies of distinguished personages lay in state in the Assembly Room, scores of forsaken dogs yapped in the city pound that was located in the cellar. Through the 1860's a refreshment stand did a brisk business in the vestibule.

In preparation for the 1876 Centennial celebrations, a committee assigned to restore Independence Hall collected more period furniture and portraits of founding fathers and rebuilt the speaker's dais in the East Room. A new bell, which still hangs in the tower, was donated by Henry Seybert, a prominent Philadelphian. Cast in Troy, New York, it weighs thirteen thousand pounds; each one thousand pounds representing one of the thirteen colonies. On its crown is inscribed the passage from St. Luke: "Glory to God in the highest, and on earth peace, good will toward men." Encircling the brim is the original quotation from Leviticus: "Proclaim Liberty throughout all the land, unto all the inhabitants thereof." In 1896, the Daughters of the American Revolution restored Independence Hall's first floor and most of the second to what they believed its appearance must have been during the Revolution.

By 1942 dingy commercial buildings crowded around historic Independence Square. The Independence Hall Association, a group involved in the movement to preserve the nation's cultural resources, determined to improve the area. To reclaim and preserve other structures significant to the story of the American nation, the Independence Historical Park Project was established and a program initiated to provide accurate restoration and refurnishing of the park buildings.

Today the four city blocks that comprise the principal section of Independence National Historical Park have been greatly enhanced. Independence Hall, having survived the years of growth of the English Colonies, the Revolution against the mother country and the establishment of a new nation, once more stands in an appropriate setting — a tangible link with the past for succeeding generations.

MIKVEH ISRAEL CEMETERY

7

Spruce Street between Eighth and Ninth. Established in 1738, this is the oldest Jewish graveyard in Philadelphia. Jewish notables of the Colonial and Revolutionary periods lie buried here, including Haym Salomon and Rebecca Gratz.

A few Jewish families had settled on the banks of the Delaware River even before William Penn arrived. Netherlands born, they had sailed across the Atlantic to colonize under the banner of the tolerant Dutch and sampled the New World first in Brazil, then in New Amsterdam in 1654, before splintering north to Rhode Island and south to that area of North America that would become Pennsylvania.

Like other seventeenth-century immigrants, men and women of the Jewish faith sought an unrestricted opportunity for a better life. In Pennsylvania they found that opportunity when, in 1681, William Penn established a commercially promising capital city of Philadelphia and set up a liberal government that guaranteed all colonists the right to own land, to do business and to hold public religious services. Jews were as free as anyone else to help populate Pennsylvania's wilderness areas or to prove their business abilities in town. Most chose the city life and took naturally to the role of small shopkeepers, land speculators and fur traders in Philadelphia.

By the early eighteenth century, Penn's country town had grown into a busy port. Jewish shopkeepers made the most of business opportunities and a number of them became prosperous merchants and ship owners. They wrote to their relatives abroad that the industrious way of life in Philadelphia suited them perfectly and pointed out that, through God's grace, they lived in peace amid Englishmen, Swedes, Germans, Scots and Welshmen who practiced the greatest variety of religions of any city in America and who all had one trait in common — a strong-willed determination to keep their own points of view.

Ambitious people streamed into Pennsylvania's capital, Jews from other colonies and Europe among them. A small religious community formed around Philadelphia's most prominent Hebrew, Nathan Levy, a ship owner who had become notable in the import-export trade. In 1738 Thomas Penn, son of William Penn, granted a piece of the open field at Ninth and Spruce Streets, then on the outskirts of town, to Nathan Levy for use as a family cemetery and to be held in trust as a "burial place for the interment of Hebrews." Five years later Levy helped organize Mikveh Israel Synagogue in a little house on Sterling Alley so that the city's Jews could worship together in the old Spanish-Portuguese (Sephardic) tradition. Such a service at Mikveh Israel was described in his journal by a visitor, J. Belnap:

Saturday, October 22, 1785: . . . Attended Sabbath Service of ye Jews . . . . When I came in the Reader was engaged in reading ye Law, having it unrolled before him on ye desk and a silver index on his hand. By his side stood two elderly men . . . looking over what he was reading . . . The rest had books in their seats on which they looked with attentiveness. After a while one of the men came from ye Reader's side and took his seat with ye rest. Then another went up and so several in procession. Between .them and ye Reader were frequent whisperings. After reading ye Law it was rolled up and ye ornaments put on (bells and ye silk tunic). Then it was held by a person who sat before ye desk while a boy of about twelve years old read in a musical voice, part of ye service in Hebrew . . .

In 1751 Nathan Levy enclosed his cemetery with a high brick wall to protect the tombstones from "many unthinking people in the habit of setting up marks [on them] and firing shots . . ." In 1777 when the British occupied Philadelphia, the Redcoats would shoot army deserters against this same wall.

Levy died in 1757 and his heirs donated the property to the congregation of Mikveh Israel Synagogue. Combined with an adjoining piece of land donated by Mathias Bush, the burial ground now measured 60 feet by 225 feet facing Spruce Street.

After Levy's death, the congregation moved to the second floor of Joseph Kauffman's house on Cherry Alley for their services. The onset of the War of Independence brought new faces into the community as "Patriot" Jews by the score left areas of the colonies now occupied by the British Army to settle in Philadelphia for the duration or to enlist there in the fighting forces. New York-born Rabbi Gershom Seixas was received in Philadelphia

Mikveh Israel Cemetery.

with joy, and he became the first official spiritual leader of Mikveh Israel. The membership, now uncomfortably crowded in Kauffman's house, voted to build a temple at Third and Cherry Streets. The synagogue, completed a year after the war's end, was paid for with the help of contributions from members of Christ Church, including Benjamin Franklin, David Rittenhouse and Charles Biddle.

In the post-Revolution years many of the men who founded Mikveh Israel were interred in the cemetery on Spruce Street. The names and dates chiseled into the old tombstones give dimension today to the story of the emerging American nation. In addition to the Nathan Levy family, the remains of Michael Gratz, his wife Miriam and their children lie there. Michael built his fortune through trade with the Indians and before the War of Independence supplied the British Colonial government with Indian goods. He was a signer of the Non-Importation Act. His son Simon helped found the Pennsylvania Academy of Fine Arts, while another son, Jacob, became a member of the Pennsylvania House of Representatives and later the State Senate.

Twenty-one Jewish soldiers of the Revolution lie near Haym Salomon in Mikveh Israel Cemetery. Salomon, broker to the Revolutionary government Office of Finance during the War of Independence, was twice imprisoned by the British in New York for assisting the escape of captured Continental soldiers and for taking part in other Sons of Liberty activities. It was resourceful Salomon who helped Robert Morris finance the war.

Benjamin Nones, who served on the staffs of both General Washington and General Lafayette, was commended for courage while under Count Pulaski's command. He became Major of the Hebrew Legion of four hundred men, and after the war was appointed an interpreter of French and Spanish for the United States government.

Phillip Moses Russel served as surgeon's mate in the Revolutionary Army and received a special commendation from General Washington for his service at Valley Forge during the winter of 1777-78.

Reuben Etting, an enlistee in the Revolutionary Army at age nineteen, suffered capture by the British at the surrender of Charleston. In 1798 he was commissioned Captain of the Independent Blues and was later appointed United States Marshall for the State of Maryland by President Jefferson.

The last of Michael and Miriam Gratz's children to be buried in the graveyard, Rebecca, achieved renown as a philanthropist whose physical, spiritual and intellectual beauty as described by Washington Irving to his friend Sir Walter Scott suggested the character of Rebecca in *Ivanhoe*.

Today the original brick wall erected in 1751 still guards Mikveh Israel cemetery from intruders. The entrance is closed by a masterfully designed iron gate, but the headstones of these Jewish-Americans of early times can still be viewed through its bars.

FRANKLIN COURT

8

South side of Market Street between Third and Fourth Streets.
The site of Benjamin Franklin's house built between 1763
and 1765, as well as three tenant houses and a print shop con-
structed by Franklin in later years.

BENJAMIN FRANKLIN, son of Josiah and Abiah Franklin, was born
in Boston in January, 1706 and trained there as a printer's apprentice.
While his father wished him to become a minister of the gospel, the boy's
avid desire to read in a diversity of subjects led both to his self-education
and to claims by worthy Bostonians that he was making "indiscreet disputa-
tions about religion." Thus in the autumn of 1723 he embarked for New
York, and finding no employment there, continued on to Philadelphia
where he established himself as a printer in his own right.

Before long he had become a leading citizen but, as he later said, he
struggled to accumulate wealth in order to have free time to be useful to
society rather than to join an aristocracy in which he had no interest. In
1731 he established a subscription library which, he later wrote, was "the
mother of all North American subscription [lending] libraries . . . " He
established the Junto, "a club of mutual improvement, in which were discussed queries on any point of morals, politics or natural philosophy."
Franklin went on to organize a fire-fighting company, a fire insurance company, an academy that later became the University of Pennsylvania, and the
Pennsylvania Hospital, the first charity hospital in America.

Franklin's inventive genius led not only to experiments with electricity, but to methods for lighting, paving and cleaning streets, the construction of an improved iron fireplace still known as the "Franklin stove," and to the placement of lightning rods on buildings. Under the pen name of "Poor Richard" he began publishing an almanac which sold some ten thousand copies each year. In it he put "the gleanings that I had made of the sense of all ages and nations." And in many colonial Pennsylvania homes, annual editions of *Poor Richard's Almanack* were the only books, other than the Bible, which a family owned.

Such activity soon brought him before the public eye, and in 1736 he was made Clerk of the Pennsylvania Assembly, a position he held until 1750 when he was elected a member. In 1737 he was appointed Postmaster of Philadelphia and by 1753 had become Deputy Postmaster-General of America, a position which enabled him to improve postal service among the colonies.

In contrast to his extensive public life, Franklin led a quiet domestic existence. He took as his common-law wife a woman named Deborah Read, whose husband had deserted her and left her unable to remarry under the laws of the colony. Shortly after their union in 1730, they accepted as their own child a son of Ben's born to a woman whose name he never revealed, and called him William, or more fondly, "Billy." Later they had two children of their own, Sarah or "Sally," and Francis who died of smallpox at the age of four. Of their early life Franklin was to write, "We kept no idle servants, our table was plain and simple, our furniture of the cheapest. For instance, my breakfast was . . . bread and milk, no tea and I ate it out of a two-penny earthen porringer with a pewter spoon . . ."

Then, in February of 1757 Franklin was appointed by the Provincial Assembly as its emissary to London. The proprietary Penn family, who no longer resided in the colony, still claimed feudal rights and refused to pay taxes on their holdings in Pennsylvania. Franklin was to present these grievances to the Penns as well as to the King and petition for the replacement of the proprietorship by a Royal government. When Ben sailed for London, Deborah remained behind to tend Sally and Mrs. Read, Deborah's mother, as well as to look after Franklin's business interests.

Franklin remained five years in England as the proceedings dragged on. While he was only partially successful in the political arena, this period enhanced Franklin's intellectual and social aspirations. He became a friend of many men of science and letters, and received an honorary degree of Doctor of Laws from Oxford University. His son William accompanied him on the trip and while in London read law at Middle Temple.

Upon his return to Philadelphia in the autumn of 1762, he saw that Deborah and their marriageable daughter Sally deserved "a good house contrived to my mind." As a prominent member of the Assembly, he himself desired a home in which he could properly entertain and where he could have room for his inventions, his books and his musical instruments.

Franklin's type composing stick (above) and the fire mark of the Philadelphia Contributionship.

Having owned property on Market Street between Third and Fourth Streets for a long time, and having gained adjacent Read family properties from his mother-in-law, who had died during his absence, Benjamin Franklin decided to build not far from the huge Philadelphia market. It pleased him to be separated only by a walled garden from the artisans and shopkeepers of the city. Enthusiastically he planned every detail of his new house down to the color of paint to be used in each room. He traveled to Perth Amboy to see William installed as Royal Governor of New Jersey and to celebrate that occasion with his son and new daughter-in-law Elizabeth. But he returned quickly to give the building commission to Philadelphia's outstanding designer, Robert Smith. In two years foundations, partitions and roof were up but much more work remained to be done before the house could be occupied.

Late in 1764, with the house partially constructed, the Assembly asked Franklin to return to London. Deborah again remained behind, this time to oversee the workmen, but much to Franklin's exasperation, she wrote him often that their home was being finished in bits and pieces. It was not until May of 1765 that Deborah and Sally could move in. In a letter written shortly afterwards, Deborah gave Ben the news that the modern scientific kitchen which her husband had designed after careful research on the physical properties of air, did not work. Ben responded:

I could have wished to be present at the Finishing of the Kitchen, as it is a mere machine, and being new to you, I think you will scarce know how to work it. The several Contrivances to carry off Steam and Smell and Smoke not being fully explain'd to you. The Oven I suppose was put up by the written Directions in my former letter. You mention of the Furnace. If that Iron One is not set, let it alone till my Return, when I shall bring a more convenient copper one.

At the end of a letter dated August, 1765 asking Deborah for more particulars about their house, Franklin turned wistful: "What Room have you chose to sleep in? I wish you could give me a particular Account of every Room, who & what is in it, t'would make me seem a little at home." Deborah replied with a long letter of October 6-13, giving the first detailed account of the almost completed house. (For clarity of reading, spelling and punctuation have been modernized in this transcript.)

Now for the room we call yours. There is in it your desk, the armonica [a musical invention of Franklin's] made like a desk, a large chest with all the writings that was in your room downstairs, the boxes of glasses for music and for the electricity, and all your clothes and pictures . . . I don't [hang them] lest it should not be right . . .

Sally has the Southroom [up] two pairs of stairs . . . The Northern room Nanney [a servant] took for her own. The Blueroom has the armonica and the harpsichord in it, the gilt sconce, a card table, a set of tea china, the worked chairs and screen, [and] a very handsome stand for the tea kettle to stand on . . . but the room is not yet finished . . . the paper has lost much of its bloom by pasting it up; therefore I thought it best to leave it 'till you come home. The curtains are not made, nor did I press for them as we have a great number of flys and it is observed they are very fond of new paint.

The Southroom I sleep in with my Susannah [her maid]. . . . In the front room which I had designed for guests I have the bed which you sent from England. In the room downstairs is the sideboard that you bespoke, which is very handsome and plain with two tables made to suit it and a dozen chairs also. The little Southroom I had papered as the walls were much soiled; in it is a pretty card table and our chairs that used to stand in the parlor and an ornamental chimney over the fireplace. On the floor is a carpet I bought cheap for the goodness; it is not quite new. The large carpet is in the Blueroom. . . .

In the Northroom we sit . . . it is not quite finished yet as the doors are not up. We have a table and chairs and a small bookcase . . . [there is] Brother John's picture and the King and Queen's picture and a small Scotch carpet on the floor . . . your time piece stands in one corner, which is all wrong, I am told. So then I tell them we shall have all things as they should be when you come home.

But more crucial matters claimed Franklin's attention in London. The colonies, increasingly irritated with British rule, were clamoring for relief from Parliament's oppressive acts. Try as he might, Franklin appeared unable to bring about a repeal of the most abhorrent restriction imposed at this time — the Stamp Act. His political enemies in Philadelphia seized upon the fact that Franklin did not seem sufficiently disturbed by the Act and that he had endorsed John Hughes, an old friend, to be distributor of the stamps in Pennsylvania. They publicly dubbed Ben Franklin a Loyalist.

Rioters threatened to attack the Franklin house in September of 1765. Governor William Franklin rushed from New Jersey to beg Deborah to come with him to Burlington. She gave Sally over to William's protection but declared herself determined to stay and defend her property. She described the ordeal in a letter to Ben:

> I was for nine days kept in continual hurry by people to remove . . . Cousin Davenport stayed with me some time. Towards nite I said he should fetch a gun or two as he had none. I sent to ask my brother to come and bring a gun also. So we turned one room into a magazine. I ordered some sort of defense upstairs such as I could manage myself.

At the last moment Joseph Galloway, leading a group of responsible citizens, broke up the mob. Philadelphians read later (when the verbatim minutes of Franklin's *Examination* by Parliament on the effects of the Stamp Act were published in America) that the great man had spoken so reasonably against the Act that his performance led to its repeal. Ashamed that they had ever doubted him, his countrymen now esteemed him more than ever.

Franklin's combined library chair and step ladder.

On November 2, 1767, her father still abroad, Sally Franklin married Richard Bache, a Philadelphia merchant. The news stirred a longing in Franklin to leave for home. Increasingly, he detected in his wife's letters that she needed him. One letter revealed that William had entertained guests in the Franklin house and Deborah had chosen to stay out of the parlor as she felt herself not "fit to be seen." It struck Ben how alone his wife must now be: Sally married, Mrs. Read dead, William in New Jersey, himself abroad and she with few friends because the taint of their common-law marriage some forty years ago still left her unacceptable to Philadelphia society.

Franklin decided to leave for home immediately. But America's handful of friends in Parliament pleaded with him not to go. England and the colonies were on the brink of war, they said, and only he, with his vision to see both sides, could prevent blunders of their government "that arise from its ignorance of America's situation" from tumbling them all into the abyss. In addition, the Pennsylvania Assembly had renewed his position as colonial agent and Georgia, New Jersey and Massachusetts also begged him to serve their interests in London.

In 1773 Deborah Franklin, an ocean away from her husband for nine years, suffered a stroke. She told William that she felt if Ben did not get back to Philadelphia that fall she would never see him again. She died December 18, 1774, and William bitterly wrote to his father that her remains had been interred in Christ Church Graveyard. Franklin's usefulness in London was now over because, as a friend wrote, "he was frequently not able to proceed for the tears literally running down his cheeks." Deborah and he had trusted and respected each other, "throve together and ever endeavored to make each other happy." In May the widower struggled home, only to learn that fighting had erupted at Lexington and Concord while he was at sea.

Scarcely had Franklin embraced Sally, his son-in-law and three grandsons, and spent a night in the house he had designed ten years earlier but never lived in, when he was appointed a member of the Pennsylvania delegation to the Second Continental Congress about to convene in the State House.

At first the seventy-year-old man felt alienated. He could only cooperate with and assist in the bold actions of the unfamiliar, angry young giants in Congress, some of whom were half his age. He kept hoping that the British would withdraw their troops and find grounds for mutual reconciliation. Franklin was well aware that the people of the colonies were by no means united in support of revolution. In addition the Continental Congress had no money nor power to tax, there was no navy, and the army consisted of an undisciplined throng led by inexperienced officers.

Finally, however, Franklin spoke out for independence. He even served on the committee to draft the Declaration of Independence and made a

few changes in Jefferson's document. Then, exhibiting his extraordinary skill at steering people around to his way of thinking, he won over the resistant Pennsylvania Assembly to the cause, warning them, "Those who would give up essential liberty to purchase a little temporary safety deserve neither liberty nor safety." Throughout the highly charged meetings that preceded the Declaration's adoption, Ben remained calm and sensible, drawing upon his never failing sense of humor to relieve the tension of angry debates.

Franklin had enjoyed his house for only a year and a half when he, along with Silas Deane and Arthur Lee, was sent by Congress to France with proposals for treaties of commerce and alliance with America. He embarked in the fall of 1776 with his grandsons William Temple Franklin and Benjamin Franklin Bache accompanying him. The leave-taking proved poignant; all realized that the success of the Revolution might depend upon the ability of America's three commissioners to persuade the French. It was a responsibility of considerable weight for Franklin, then in his seventy-first year.

Upon reaching Paris, Franklin established himself in a house at Passy, then a suburb, and almost immediately became a part of the high society life in the court of Louis XVI and Marie Antoinette. Even before Franklin's arrival, secret aid was being sent by French Foreign Minister Vergennes through an agent, the noted author Beaumarchais, who concealed his operations under the name "Roderigue Hortalez & Company." From a Paris warehouse, large quantities of munitions and clothing were finding their way to America and into the hands of Marie Antoinette's "dear Republicans."

But Vergennes wisely held back open hostility against the British until the strength and temper of the American "rebels" had been tested. General Howe's army pressed into Philadelphia in the fall of 1777 while George Washington and his men went to Valley Forge. Franklin's house was taken over by British General Sir Charles Grey and officers of his regiment and Sally and Richard Bache fled to the country with their children. The following summer, after the British had left the city, Franklin received word that some musical instruments, books and electrical apparatus were carried off and that "a Captain André took with him a picture of you [by Benjamin Wilson] which hung in the dining room."

Meanwhile, in Paris Franklin and the commissioners sought to gain as much indirect assistance as possible. Then, in December, 1777 came the news of Burgoyne's surrender of British troops at Saratoga the preceding October. France was now willing to throw her full support behind the American cause, and in February, 1778 formal treaties of alliance and commerce were signed, granting the Americans financial and military support, as well as a supply of arms, clothing and other badly needed provisions.

England surrendered at Yorktown in October, 1781 to a combined

Entrance to Franklin Court (from a drawing by William M. Campbell).

French and American force and a formal treaty of peace was signed in 1783, but it was not until 1785 that Benjamin Franklin was granted permission by Congress to "return to America as soon as convenient." On September 13 he arrived home to be greeted with a roaring hero's welcome.

Almost immediately he was elected a member of the Pennsylvania State Council and shortly after became its President. To the amazement of many, though in poor health, Franklin accepted the demanding position. On the day of election the aching old man, clad in a black velvet suit, led the procession from the State House to the Court House a few blocks away and climbed "a considerable number of steps to be proclaimed by common cry." That at his age he would take on the burden of a faction-ridden Council some politicians said was a sure sign of senility, and Franklin seemed to agree. He wrote:

> I had not firmness enough to resist the unanimous desire of my country-folks; and I find myself harnessed again in their service. They engrossed the prime of my life. They have eaten my flesh, and seem resolved now to pick my bones.

His advanced years, however, did not keep Dr. Franklin from engineering extensive alterations to his house, which at this point had grown too noisy and crowded with Sally and Richard's children for his comfort. He built an addition to the main house which included a wood cellar, a dining room to seat twenty-four people, a library, two bedrooms and a garret. He also built three tenant houses on Market Street and a print shop for his grandson Benjamin Franklin Bache.

By now the pain from a "stone" which had troubled him over the years could only be helped by soaking in a warm bath for hours every day. His tub was slipper-shaped and made of copper. He sometimes entertained friends while sitting in the heel of it with his legs under the vamp. Across the vamp he had a place to rest his book and friends reported, "There he sits and enjoys himself."

In 1787 the Constitutional Convention met in Philadelphia to revise the Articles of Confederation and Benjamin Franklin, one of four members who had signed the Declaration of Independence, served as a delegate from Pennsylvania. He found the convention the most august and respectable assembly he had ever attended. As President of Pennsylvania he entertained many of the fifty-five delegates at his home that summer. George Washington found him in his walled garden sitting on a grass plot under a very large mulberry tree. Manasseh Cutler described his visit with the "trunched old man" surrounded by several other members of the convention and two or three ladies:

> The tea table was spread under the trees and Mrs. Bache [Sally Franklin], a very gross and rather homely lady . . . served it . . . She had three of her children around her, over whom she seemed to have no kind of command, but who appeared excessively fond of their grandpa.

After it turned dark, Cutler went into Franklin's library:

> The largest and by far the best private library in America. He showed us a glass machine for exhibiting the circulation of the blood in the arteries and veins . . . a rolling press for taking copies of letters in less than two minutes . . . his long artificial arm and hand for taking down . . . books and his great armed chair with rocker . . . with which he fans himself with only a small motion of his foot, and many other curiosities and inventions.

Franklin's term in Council now over, he looked forward to spending the rest of his days in repose which, for him, meant books, grandchildren and gardens, cards and a sampling of "balls, concerts and little parties . . . in which there is frequently good music and sometimes dancing." In 1790, three weeks before his death, he wrote his last public paper, *An Address to the Public from the Pennsylvania Society for Promoting the Abolition of Slavery*. As President of the Abolition Society, Franklin signed a memorandum asking for the discouragement of the slave trade. Thomas Jefferson visited him toward the end of May and on April 2 wrote the Comtesse d'Houdetot in Paris, "I found our friend Dr. Franklin in his bed, cheerful, but still in his bed. He took a lively interest in the details I gave him of your revolution. I observed his face often flush in the course of it. He is much emaciated." Ten days before his death he sat for his portrait by

Charles Willson Peale who described him as "confined to his room in much pain which he bore with philosophical countenance . . . his grey locks . . . grown long and undulating gracefully over his shoulders contrasting well with his bald head."

Three days before his death he dictated a letter to Jefferson, after which he got out of bed and asked Sally to make it up so that he might be able to "die in a decent manner." His daughter said she hoped he'd live for many years longer, to which he responded, "I hope not." Then having settled back into bed, she advised him to change position in order to breathe easy. He commented, "A dying man can do nothing easy."

On April 17, 1790, with grandsons at his bedside, eighty-four-year-old Benjamin Franklin "gave a sigh, breathed a few seconds and died without pain." Franklin's funeral drew into the streets of Philadelphia a crowd described by the newspapers as "an immense concourse of people." Thirty clergymen attended the body to Christ Church graveyard where he was laid to rest beside Deborah. All the bells in the city tolled a muffled peal and "nothing was omitted that could show the respect and veneration of his fellow citizens for so great a character." The community of Paris and the National Assembly sent letters of condolence — the first instance of homage being paid by a public body of one nation to a private citizen of another.

Following Franklin's death the house was left to the Baches who in turn rented it to a succession of tenants, including Chevalier de Friere, Portuguese Minister to the United States from 1794 to 1799. By 1803 the house had become the Franklin Coffee House and Hotel. Sally and Richard Bache returned there in 1808 and she died in that same year. After Sally's death the American Free School occupied the building until its demolition in 1812.

The property now known as Franklin Court was acquired by the National Park Service in 1948. Archaeological excavations started in 1953 uncovered some original foundations of the house, necessaries and artifacts. A multimedia exhibit to tell the story of Benjamin Franklin — the man of many facets — is planned for this site. Among other displays there will be an eighteenth-century working printing press and an operating post office.

CARPENTERS' HALL AND COURT 9

320 Chestnut Street between Third and Fourth Streets. Carpenters' Hall was erected in 1770-1774 by the Carpenters' Company which still owns and maintains it. The First Continental Congress met in 1774. The Court also includes Pemberton House built in 1775, and New Hall constructed in 1791 by the Carpenters' Company, both of which are now reconstructed and house military museums.

IN Pennsylvania's earliest days, skilled artisans comprised the bulk of Philadelphia's population; many were bricklayers, stonecutters or carpenters, who followed Quaker leader William Penn from England, seeking both religious freedom and employment opportunities in the New World.

Over a period of forty years, through dawn-to-dusk labors, these craftsmen built hundreds of neat brick houses on the west bank of the Delaware River and won for Philadelphia the reputation of being "the best built city in the British colonies." By 1724 master carpenters had achieved sufficient prestige and wealth to spend some hours away from the scaffolds, bettering themselves and helping their fellows. They formed the Carpenters' Company of the City and County of Philadelphia, "for the purpose of obtaining instruction in the science of architecture [to this time architecture had been an intellectual pursuit for gentlemen] and assisting such of their members as should by accident be in need of support or the widows and minor children of members. . . ."

Entrance to Carpenters' Hall and Court.

In 1770 when the Carpenters' Company had been in existence almost fifty years and Philadelphia was experiencing America's first building boom, the membership voted to construct a hall in which they could meet and transact their business. They bought a long, narrow piece of property south of Chestnut Street between Third and Fourth, away from the noise of the dock area and convenient to new houses on Walnut and Chestnut Streets and to the State House, center of municipal and provincial government. Here they developed a court as a setting for their hall and connected it to Chestnut Street by a footpath along which they could, at a future date, erect buildings as rent producers.

The man chosen from the Carpenters' Company to design Carpenters' Hall was the genial owner of Buck Tavern, master carpenter Robert Smith, already known as one of America's most successful "architects." Smith had designed the Christ Church steeple, Princeton University's Nassau Hall (which set the pattern for Harvard's Hollis Hall, Brown's University Hall and Dartmouth Hall), St. Peter's Church in Philadelphia, New College of Pennsylvania, Benjamin Franklin's house on High Street, the Third Presbyterian Church, Philadelphia's Bettering House and the Zion Lutheran Church. In 1774 he would build Philadelphia's Walnut Street Prison, remarkable for its fireproof construction.

Smith supplied the plans while other members provided material and labor for Carpenters' Hall. Journeymen began construction in 1770 and finished it in 1774. Carpenters' Hall, standing at the end of Carpenters' Court, presented a pleasing picture to the eye. The two-story, cross-shaped brick structure crowned by a cupola gave the impression of having four facades. The vigorous woodwork, both inside and out, exhibited the craftsmanship of Philadelphia carpenters. An entry divided the first floor interior into two rooms. The second floor, designed for the Library Company which had been crowded in one room of the State House, consisted of a reading room and a directors' meeting room, both heated by open fireplaces and lit by candles. Inside shutters insulated the rooms against drafts and books on the shelves were protected by wire lattice work.

The Company sold a third of the Chestnut Street frontage to Joseph Pemberton, a Quaker merchant, who constructed a home there in 1775. The effect of this ". . . large, elegant and commodius new brick house . . ." was an architectural frame which screened Carpenters' Hall from view except through the entrance of the court. The three-story home was finished and furnished more richly than most of Philadelphia's brick row houses and reflected the wealth, pretensions and ambitions of its owner. It also may have contributed to his downfall, for shortly after the house was completed, Pemberton declared bankruptcy and sold the house to another merchant, William Sykes, who lived there for the next thirteen years.

In the spring of 1774, strained relations between Great Britain and her American colonies worsened. When Paul Revere brought the news to

Philadelphians that the British had closed the port of Boston to all shipping but food and fuel, an outraged crowd gathered at City Tavern to debate how men who knew their rights should react. Several of the colonies already had formed Committees of Correspondence to improve communications between provinces. Philadelphia's immediate response to the Boston blockade was to form such a committee and draft a letter of sympathy to the people of Boston.

Until this time, no country in the world had ever consulted "mechanics" about government affairs. But the Boston boycott of British goods was "carried through and organized by the venerable orders of men styled mechanics and husbandmen." Newspaper editors pointed to the appropriateness of this participation, for certainly mechanics and laborers suffered just as much from oppressive taxation as lawyers and merchants. They kept their eyes on Philadelphia's Carpenters' Company, considered the most influential and best organized of the industrial bodies in the colonies, as it threw all its strength behind Patriot committees and its leading members stepped into the revolutionary whirlwind.

Robert Smith, first appointed to a committee to correspond with the mechanics of New York City, soon moved up to a larger committee to correspond with sister colonies, urging that they "prepare for local defense and send relief to occupied Boston." This committee also recommended the organization of an inter-colonial congress to meet in Philadelphia in September of 1774.

All that summer of 1774, anti-British activists assembled in the only privately owned hall in Philadelphia — Carpenters'. Workmen in Howell's Tanyard, just south of the Company's property, could hear rousing speeches through the hall's open windows. Loyalist newspapers criticized the carpenter-landlords for offering a platform for "traitorous noise" against England, but the carpenters ignored their threats. When fifty-six delegates to the First Continental Congress arrived that September, the Carpenters' Company offered them use of their hall. Representatives included Samuel and John Adams from Massachusetts and Patrick Henry from Virginia, who believed in resisting Britain by every means short of war and who were shunned at the time by most colonists for being too radical. The conservatives of the Congress were led by Joseph Galloway of Pennsylvania.

Galloway, Speaker of Pennsylvania's Provincial Assembly, offered the State House to the Continental Congress for its meeting, claiming that it seemed more appropriate than a carpenters' hall. But the other delegates, aware that the perturbed colonies were rapidly growing more democratic and that popular opinion held "mechanics and husbandmen" as "the strength of every community," delayed their decision until they could walk from City Tavern, scene of their preliminary gathering, to Carpenters' Hall to look at the building. In John Adams' words, "The general cry was that this is a good room," and they voted to hold their sessions there.

The purpose of the First Continental Congress was to consult. For seven weeks the delegates, led by their President, Peyton Randolph, declared the colonies' rights and voted their grievances. They commended the resistance of Massachusetts against the punitive Intolerable Acts, put an embargo on British goods and took a step toward union among the colonies by forming an association under which would be organized committees of safety and inspection to carry out their policies. Before ice and snow could block the roads and waterways, the delegates left Philadelphia for home, vowing to assemble again the next May if their Petition to the King had not been acted upon and a "redress of grievances" obtained before that time.

Fighting broke out in Massachusetts in April, 1775, and Philadelphia feared for the security of its port. Robert Smith devised an apparatus made of logs and weighted down with ballast to keep enemy ships from stealing up the Delaware. The master carpenter contributed his free services to supervise its construction, and when it was installed in the river the following year, it successfully blocked the enemy from entry.

The Second Continental Congress, which met in Philadelphia in 1775, held its sessions in the State House, while other committees used Carpenters' Hall. By May of 1776, many of the colonies had expressed willingness to commit themselves to independence from Britain. But Pennsylvania's provincial government would not commit a disloyalty to the King, despite the readiness of its German and Scotch-Irish population to fight and the growing sympathy in Philadelphia for the cause. The frustrated Congress, in what John Adams called "a decisive event," finally urged the people of all the colonies "to assume all the powers of government," and a new People's Government of Pennsylvania gathered at Carpenters' Hall, where it agreed to follow the others in seeking independence from England.

The outbreak of the War of Independence found members of the Carpenters' Company building defense networks, barracks and forts on the New Jersey side of the Delaware as well as in the Philadelphia area. Cannon rumbled close to Philadelphia in 1777. The cellar of Carpenters' Hall was opened for storage of Army goods and soon the first floor became an infirmary for disabled soldiers. It continued as a hospital even after the British occupied the city and, after the Revolution, became a repository for "trophies of war." The free-thinking Unitarians that English refugee scientist Joseph Priestley helped to establish a church, met in Carpenters' Hall for several years, starting in 1796.

In 1856 the Carpenters' Company, always sensitive to its historic associations, renovated Carpenters' Hall, "being careful to preserve as much as possible every feature . . . indicative of its original finish." A remarkable pioneer work of preservation, the hall has been carefully maintained by the Carpenters' Company ever since as an historic shrine.

Following the Revolution, the nation entered a period of prosperity. Carpenters' Company was successful in renting its entire building to the

First Bank of the United States, and in 1791 decided to build a two-story brick building as a meeting place for its members on land adjacent to Carpenters' Hall. Called "New Hall," it was located on the west side of Carpenters' Court, only a few feet from the temporary home of the monetary center of the United States. New Hall was 61 feet along the court by 20 feet in depth, and consisted of two stories and a cellar. The second floor had one "long room" which the Carpenters' Company used for its meetings.

The first floor was rented to the U.S. War Department. Beginning in November 1791 and continuing for about two years, Secretary of War, General Henry Knox, directed the Department with an office staff of five from this building. Knox was a trusted adviser to President Washington and advocate of a number of projects promoting efficiency in the military arts for the benefit of the Republic. During the last decade of the eighteenth century and also in the nineteenth century numerous social, cultural, religious and educational organizations rented space in New Hall.

In the 1850's, two stories were added to New Hall. Over the years, the building underwent extensive repairs and in 1958 the structure, then in a very poor condition with little of the original building intact, was torn down. Reconstruction began shortly thereafter with funds donated by the Louise Curtis Foundation. Since June, 1965 a military museum commemorating the events of the United States Marine Corps during the last quarter of the eighteenth century has been housed here.

Pemberton House was sold by Edward Tilghman to David Kennedy in 1800 and shortly after, two stories were added to the building. From 1816 until 1823 Richard Bache, grandson of Benjamin Franklin, operated the Philadelphia post office from the structure. In 1840 it was demolished and replaced by a new building which, in turn, was razed one hundred years later. In 1968 Pemberton House was reconstructed with funds provided by the Army Association and Navy League, and now houses the Army-Navy Museum which depicts the growth of the U.S. military and naval forces from 1775 to 1800.

DESHLER-MORRIS HOUSE

10

5442 Germantown Avenue, Germantown. Built by David Deshler in 1772-73 as a country residence, this house served British Commander Sir William Howe as his headquarters during the Battle of Germantown in 1777 and President George Washington as a "Summer White House" in 1793 and 1794.

ON the evening of the fourth of October, 1777, a Germantown resident by the name of John Miller scratched in his diary with a trembling hand, "This morning I returned from town to find a hot engagement had been here between the American Army and that of the British where many on both sides are slain. Poor Mrs. Miller was alone upstairs when a cannon ball passed through a window very near her."

The colonies and England had been at war for more than two years, but until this day the people who lived in Germantown, a village eight miles outside of Philadelphia, had seen little bloodshed. But on this day the wounded soldiers moaning in the dirt lanes beneath their windows horrified the townspeople, many of them Quakers. They had already sent an entreaty to the leaders of both sides to lay down their arms. But Chief of the British Army, Sir William Howe, and General George Washington had ignored the plea.

Philadelphia had been occupied by British troops under the command of Lord Cornwallis on September 26, a day on which "bands struck up the tune of 'God Save the King' amidst the acclaimations of several thousand

Bedroom used by George Washington in the Deshler-Morris House.

[Loyalist] inhabitants." Meanwhile, Howe had stationed the main body of his army at Germantown and General Washington was encamped at Skippack Creek.

On October third, having learned that Howe had dispatched part of his force to Philadelphia, Washington ordered a night march to attack Germantown at daybreak. But the morning of the fourth found the area enshrouded in thick fog, a distinct advantage for the well-disciplined British. Nevertheless, Washington pressed his men into action and for two hours a violent battle raged. Then, for reasons that are still not entirely clear, both sides disengaged. Washington retreated to Skippack, and soon after led his men to Valley Forge. Had Howe pursued the Americans and forced a full scale engagement, the outcome of the Revolution might have been different. In the future Howe would never again have the same opportunity.

While in Germantown, the British general had commandeered the handsome country residence on Market Square owned by David Deshler for his headquarters. A successful West Indian merchant in Philadelphia, Deshler had chosen Germantown for the setting of his country home four years earlier. The village enjoyed the reputation of being a pleasant and healthful retreat on high ground, away from the dust and traffic of populous Philadelphia. A number of well-to-do city families passed their summers there among the craftsmen and farmers, many of whom were German immigrants.

Deshler purchased two acres of ground overlooking Market Square and constructed a house said to be the finest example of Georgian architecture in Germantown, "finished in the most elegant manner" with a carriage house, a stable and a "water pump in the yard." He planted a vineyard, an orchard and a garden that grew to be a "marvel of the region." The local Quaker children in conservative garb at first fell back at the sight of the new neighbor clad in green velvet with silver buckles. But soon they earned more than a penny helping him stock his cellar with bottles of wine, produce from the local farms, salted meats and game fowl. Their parents found Deshler "honest," and when he lined the shelves of his 32-foot-long entrance hall with books on many subjects, including medicine (in which he dabbled), even the schoolmaster who lived nearby labeled him a worthy gentleman of refined tastes.

David Deshler died in 1792, eleven years after America won her independence from England and two years after Philadelphia had become the temporary capital of the United States. Colonel David Franks, a gentleman of the Jewish faith and a veteran officer of the Revolutionary Army who had served under George Washington, bought the merchant's property. Franks, who had been wounded three times, found an ironic triumph in possessing the very house from which General Howe had directed British forces during the battle of Germantown.

Franks had occupied the Deshler house less than a year when the "contagious and mortal" yellow fever epidemic of 1793 drove thousands of Philadelphians to seek the clean air of Germantown. Even George Washington, now the first President of the United States and headquartered in Philadelphia, dared not brave the "strange and melancholy" metropolis with the pall of death upon it. He sent word to his heads of departments that so long as government must go on, the Cabinet would meet in November in Germantown, and that they should lose no time finding lodging there.

Secretary of State Thomas Jefferson, first to respond to the President's order, could find nothing better in the crowded refuge than "a bed in the public room of a tavern." And he wrote a warning to James Madison that he might "not be able to get even a half bed, should he not come right away." Washington, meanwhile, arranged with Colonel Franks to rent his house, since of the places suggested to him this one appeared "more commodious for myself and the entertainment of company."

Four Cabinet meetings took place in David Franks' home in November in the large room to the left of the entrance hall. Before returning to Philadelphia when the first frost halted the epidemic, the President gave two dinners for the Cabinet at a table set with Mrs. Franks' seventy-two-piece Nanking china. Washington hired a cook and a baker, both citizens of Germantown, for the occasions.

The following summer the President rented Franks' home again. He had found it comfortable and unostentatious and he saw in it an ideal retreat for his wife Martha and their adopted children, Eleanor Parke Custis and George Washington Custis. The President wanted to spend the summer with his family, yet he felt he dared not be far from the government, where he must attend to the serious "Whiskey Rebellion," then a threatening disorder. During the summer of 1794, Washington used two rooms of the Franks' house more than any others; the small second floor chamber adjoining the master bedroom where he enjoyed perfect quiet to work on state papers, and the cozy breakfast parlor that always seemed redolent with the aroma of cinnamon and roasting apples, and where he could stand with his back to the tile-framed fireplace and view the orchard.

That summer Washington found time to pose for his portrait. After asking him to remove his lower porcelain teeth and insert a wad of cotton to fill out the lower lip for a more natural look, artist Gilbert Stuart painted the father of the nation. Martha Washington delighted in the garden. She raised hyacinths under globes of cut glass, six of which she took to the daughter of the deceased David Deshler when she returned to Philadelphia.

George Washington and his family stayed in Germantown from July 30 to September 20, 1794. Once back in Philadelphia he paid Colonel Franks $201.60 for the rental of furniture, bedding, china and the loss of "one flat iron, large fork, four plates, three ducks, four fowls, one bushel of potatoes and one hundred pounds of hay."

Colonel David Franks sold the house built by David Deshler to Elliston and John Perot in 1804. When Elliston died thirty-three summers later, his daughter's husband, Samuel Morris, bought it. The house remained in the Morris family until it was willed to the United States government in 1948.

The Deshler-Morris house is the last remaining residence, other than Mount Vernon, which served as George Washington's abode for any considerable time.

CITY TAVERN

11

Second Street between Walnut and Chestnut Streets. Completed in 1773, this City Hotel was a favorite meeting place of the men who founded the American government.

IN the first half of the eighteenth century Philadelphia had become a city of some forty thousand people. Colorful wooden signs on almost every street corner marked houses licensed to sell food, drink, spirits and lodging to local people, to travelers who stopped off on their way to other colonies, and to the many immigrants for whom the city was port of entry to America.

By 1758 public houses numbered a staggering 117, all somewhat rough and provincial in the opinion of the newly emerged social elite of Philadelphia, and unworthy of the second largest metropolis in the British Empire. With a new perspective gained from education and travel in Europe, these prestigious citizens claimed that the time had come for a "genteel accommodation . . . which would offer a spacious room in which concerts and operas could be presented and balls and banquets held."

In 1772, a group led by Governor John Penn, Chief Justice Benjamin Chew and John Dickinson subscribed funds for a non-profit City Tavern, "for the convenience and credit of the city," which would be "the most . . . elegant structure of its kind in America." The handsome brick building rose in 1773 on a lot on the west side of Second Street above Walnut.

The trustees, departing from the customary arrangement of an inn-keeper with his wife in the kitchen and other relatives performing menial tasks, employed an experienced Englishman named Daniel Smith to serve as City Tavern's overseer. Smith equipped and furnished the place in the "English style." He hired a bartender and chef and advertised in the newspapers: "Large and small parties or single gentlemen [served] breakfast, dinner or supper at hours most convenient to themselves, soups, jellies and ice creams, the prime and earliest produce of the season, a cold buffet and a selection of spirituous and malt liquors from London and other breweries . . . and a variety of French liquors. . . ."

City Tavern was an instant success, for in addition to food, drink and lodging, it offered Philadelphians a social center it had never had before. Merchants and ship captains talked business in rooms on the ground floor, treated each other to refreshments and punch, and studied lists furnished by the management of the latest market prices and ship movements. Other gentlemen relaxed over coffee and all could obtain newspapers at the bar.

The second floor of City Tavern offered rooms for meetings or private dinners and a long, narrow room the width of the building which was capable of accommodating one hundred people at a banquet. This "Long Room" quickly became the new home for the Philadelphia Dancing Assembly whose fortnightly dances to minuets and quadrilles kept third-floor lodgers awake until two in the morning. A piazza extended along the rear of City Tavern with a porch beneath and stairs leading down to kitchens and store rooms in the cellar.

The men who developed City Tavern hoped that it would become a center where political, commercial and literary as well as religious issues "would be . . . earnestly discussed." Their wish came true as the feelings of the colonists against British Parliament became more belligerent and the politics of protest dominated all conversation at City Tavern. The climactic "discussion" took place after Paul Revere galloped into Philadelphia early in 1774 with the news that Britain had closed the port of Boston.

Then two hundred outraged Whigs, Tories and representatives of the Proprietary Party jammed into the Long Room of City Tavern. Over the noise of the crowd, John Dickinson put forth some calm and moderate proposals, but angry Charles Thomson spoke his mind so vehemently against Parliament that he fainted and had to be carried into another room to recover. The meeting ended with all in "tolerable good humor." Despite disagreements, they had appointed a committee to convey sympathy to Bostonians, to suggest "firmness, prudence and moderation" in the crisis, and to assure them of Philadelphia's "firm adherence to the cause of American liberty."

The next morning the Committee of Correspondence wrote to the southern colonies suggesting that a "congress of delegates from all the colonies meet and devise measures for the common safety." From Williamsburg the call went out to the other colonies and by late August delegates to the First Continental Congress began to arrive in Philadelphia.

City Tavern (from a Birch engraving of 1800).

On August 29, 1774, a party of dignitaries rode out to greet the anxiously awaited New England delegation — among them Samuel Adams and John Adams of Massachusetts — and conduct them into town where, as John Adams wrote in his diary that night, "Dirty, dusty and fatigued as we were, we could not resist the importunity to go to the tavern, the most genteel one in America. . . . Here . . . after some time spent in conversation, a curtain was drawn in the other half of the chamber, a supper appeared as elegant as ever laid upon a table. . . ."

City Tavern became the first gathering place for the Continental Congress. Delegates got acquainted over food and drink and calculated who would be friend and who foe to their individual views. Colonel George Washington of Virginia even arranged to dine there regularly in "a club."

From the beginning, the atmosphere at City Tavern was electric. The first clash between radicals and conservatives took place almost immediately over a choice of a meeting hall and conservative Speaker of the Pennsylvania Assembly Joseph Galloway's invitation to use the Assembly Room of the State House was declined in favor of Carpenters' Hall.

It took nearly two months for the First Continental Congress to hammer out a Petition to the King which included a declaration of rights. The emotionally drained delegates were dined and wined at farewell "entertainments" at City Tavern before they left for home.

King George turned a deaf ear to Congress' petition, and relations between England and the colonies continued to decline. The Second Continental Congress convened in Philadelphia. This time the delegates met in the State House and caucused in the private club rooms of City Tavern where all dined together each Saturday. On other nights a table was reserved regularly for Randolph, Lee, Harrison and Washington of Virginia, Alsop of New York, Chase of Maryland and Rodney and Read of Delaware. The Continental Congress adopted the Declaration of Independence on July 4, 1776 and the colonies found themselves plunged into a revolution.

Congress, along with military officers, celebrated the first anniversary of the adoption of the Declaration of Independence in 1777 at City Tavern while bonfires and fireworks lit the summer sky outside. But two months later it was a different story when British troops occupied Philadelphia and Congress was forced to flee.

For the British the occupation of Philadelphia turned out to be a pleasant duty. Fawned upon by thousands of Loyalists gathered there, many of whom came from other colonies, the polished young officers danced at one extravagant ball after another in City Tavern and made their conquests among Tory belles. General Howe and his men trooped out of Philadelphia in June of 1778, followed by an exodus of three thousand Loyalists. An almost powerless Congress limped back to the State House where it resumed its struggle to assert authority over the thirteen bickering colonies and obtain money to pay the Continental soldiers.

That their ragged fighting men were in desperate need of supplies scarcely tweaked the consciences of some of Philadelphia's "Patriots" who felt that they owed it to themselves to throw off the gloom of the occupation year. In a rash of celebrations, including one to honor the French Alliance and another for General Washington who arrived in 1779 for a month of consultations with Congress, they held many gala evenings at City Tavern. Washington's aide-de-camp, Lieutenant General Nathaniel Greene, exhausted by it all, recorded his ordeal:

. . . I spent a month in the most agreeable and disagreeable manner I ever did . . . in my life. We had the most splendid entertainment imaginable; large assemblies, evening balls etc. It was hard service to go through the duties of the day. I was obliged to rise early and go to bed late to complete them. In the morning a round of visiting came on. Then you had to prepare for dinner, after which the evening balls would engage your time until one or two in the morning . . . the exhibition was such a scene of luxury and profusion they gave . . . more pain than pleasure.

Such lavish display at City Tavern disgusted a good number of citizens who worried over the precarious state of finances in 1779. One man wrote, "Entertainments, assemblies, balls! The extravagance . . . is very unfriendly to a Republican government and greatly unnerves the national strength."

Still, some Philadelphians pursued their social life with a vengeance, inviting French and Spanish dignitaries to join them at City Tavern. The sophisticated French Marquis de Castellux was amused by the earnest participants in the Dancing Assemblies of 1789, who turned a delightful pastime into a rigid exercise. He described one master of ceremonies at an Assembly Ball who barked at a damsel permitting a bit of gossip to interrupt her turn in a contradance: "Come, Miss, have a care what you are doing. Do you think you are here for your own pleasure?"

The War of the Revolution climaxed in a decisive victory for the Americans at Yorktown in 1781 and a treaty of peace was signed in 1783. General George Washington agreed to serve as President of the convention which met in the State House four years later to revise the Articles of Confederation. While in town he again passed his evenings at City Tavern, dining with friends and attending concerts. As President-elect of the United States in April of 1789, his triumphal entry into Philadelphia while on route to New York City was capped by a dinner at City Tavern for two hundred and fifty people.

The federal government, when it sat in New York, named Philadelphia the temporary capital of the United States and moved there late in 1790. Old-time Congressmen returning to the city found that City Tavern was no longer the glamorous place they remembered. It had become more a commercial establishment, popularly known as the Merchants' Coffee House, where businessmen assembled every day at two o'clock "to find out current market values, to learn . . . ship movements in the port [noted in the register] and to hear the news." An agent left each day to go down the river to New Castle for the latest information on ship arrivals and departures.

That it had become a very useful establishment, no one could doubt. City Tavern, now a coffee house, even had a room for the underwriting of insurance. But many people of refined tastes now found it "noisy and disagreeable." The Dancing Assembly moved to other quarters and only a few of the congressmen rented rooms in the old hostelry, even though at fifteen dollars a week the management had promised to pay "special attention to cleanliness."

A disastrous fire damaged the building in 1834, causing the merchants to shift their activities one block away to the new Exchange at Third and Walnut Streets. Repairs were made, but the old City Tavern-Merchants' Coffee House began a long downward slide. Soon it could attract no more genteel a tenant than an auctioneer and a pawnbroker who advertised, "All business transactions strictly confidential. Private entrance from the back alley." In 1854 the old structure, once the social center of the founders of the nation, was razed to make way for buildings emblematic of another period. City Tavern will be reconstructed and refurnished to function as an operating eighteenth-century tavern by 1976.

Lap desk used by Thomas Jefferson when he wrote the Declaration of Independence.

GRAFF HOUSE

12

700-Market Street. A reconstruction of the home erected on this site in 1775 by Jacob Graff, Jr. It was here that Thomas Jefferson drafted the Declaration of Independence in June of 1776.

INCREASING political unrest in the colonies in 1775 did not deter the industrious citizens of the populous port city of Philadelphia from their usual pursuit of food, shelter and the improvement of their situations. In June of that year Jacob Graff, Jr., a bricklayer, bought a piece of ground on the southwest corner of Seventh and Market Streets from Edmund Physick and built a house for his wife, baby son Frederick and himself.

The Graff house was a modest brick structure that resembled many other homes rising in the vicinity of the State House. Measuring seventeen feet on Market Street by fifty feet on Seventh Street, it contained two rooms separated by a central stair hall on each of its three floors, and provided enough chambers for the family, plus two to rent out for additional income, should the need arise.

In the winter of 1775, the rift having widened between Britain and America, patriots from as far away as Boston to the north and Williamsburg to the south slipped in and out of local taverns to pass on news of the latest activity of the Sons of Liberty or huddle over Thomas Paine's plea for freedom, *Common Sense,* which was "working a powerful change in the minds of men." These activists and other strangers brought to Philadelphia by the crisis filled every bed in the inns. That spring even

City Tavern, Philadelphia's new "genteel" accommodation, overflowed with delegates to the Second Continental Congress, bent on decisive measures. The delegates who could not obtain rooms at City Tavern looked to private homes for lodging. It was then that Jacob Graff let it be known that he would take a boarder.

Thomas Jefferson, a delegate from Virginia to the Continental Congress, hooked his long fingers around the knocker on the door of the Seventh Street entrance to the Graffs' house and applied for the rooms. A handsome, raw-boned man in his thirties, six feet two inches tall, he stooped to enter. He assured the Graffs that his requirements were simple; just a furnished bedroom and a parlor in which he could write uninterrupted, a habit he had developed in his youth. He would not fail to pay his rent, he promised, nor would he entertain ladies or keep the Graffs' baby awake with overhead noise from a gathering of politicians. He appreciated privacy.

The Graffs rented their second-floor rooms to Jefferson and the lawyer transferred his belongings from Benjamin Randolph's house, where Jefferson had stayed temporarily on his arrival and where he had quartered for three months of the previous year while attending the first session of the Second Continental Congress.

Jacob Graff did not realize at first that his tenant was "one of the strongest members" of Congress. He could not imagine why the gentleman burned his candles so late every night in June. The truth of the matter was that on June 11, shortly after Jefferson moved in, Congress had nominated him one of a five-man committee to prepare a formal statement justifying independence for the colonies. Benjamin Franklin, John Adams, Robert R. Livingston and Roger Sherman had also been named to the committee. Aware that the Virginia lawyer already had demonstrated his rhetoric as early as 1774 in a paper entitled, *A Summary View of the Rights of British America* and had just completed a draft of the Virginia Constitution, the committee gave the job almost completely to Thomas Jefferson.

Jefferson retired to his parlor at the Graff house, rolled up the sleeves of his linen shirt and seated himself by the open window where cool night air circulated. He worked on a lap-desk made to his specifications the previous year by Mr. Randolph, who was a cabinetmaker. Though his thoughts fairly tumbled from the quill pen to the paper, it took many long hours to arrange them in proper order and to word them in a graceful style.

When finished, Jefferson held in his hand the document which would become the first formal assertion by a whole people of their right to a government of their own choice. The paper included at least one immortal statement:

We the people hold these truths to be sacred and undeniable, that all men are created equal, that they are endowed by their Creator with certain unalienable Rights, that among these are Life, Liberty and the pursuit of Happiness. That to secure these rights, Governments are instituted among Men, deriving their just powers from the consent of the governed . . .

Having completed the first draft of the Declaration to his own satisfaction, Jefferson submitted the paper to the other committee members. In its wording they recognized a document superbly fitted to the purpose. Franklin substituted "self-evident" for "sacred and undeniable," but other than that the committee made only a few minor changes and the Declaration was presented to Congress for its approval.

As is often the case when a body of individuals with differing points of view attempt to agree on a statement expressing their common interest, various members sought to have specific passages altered or deleted. The delegates from South Carolina and Georgia insisted that Jefferson's denunciation of slavery be omitted on the grounds that England was not responsible for slave trade in the colonies and the point merely clouded the issue. Other sections which were of a highly personal nature to Jefferson also were deleted. One in particular clearly shows the terrible conflict faced not only by Jefferson, but by thousands of individuals who had close ties with families and friends in England. Toward the end of his first draft, Jefferson had written:

These facts have given the last stab to agonizing affection, and manly spirit bids us to renounce forever these unfeeling brethren. We must endeavor to forget our former love for them, and to hold them as we might hold the rest of mankind, enemies in war, in peace friends. We might have been a free and great people together.

On July 4, 1776 Jefferson's Declaration with revisions by Congress was voted upon and unanimously passed. On July 8, the Declaration was publicly proclaimed in the State House Yard. Jefferson's feelings at the time, however, could be described as unhappy at the "mutilations" Congress had made in his document, and he sent copies to his friends asking them if they did not prefer the original version.

Actually very few Americans outside of Congress knew the identity of the author of the Declaration of Independence until almost three years after the war. Toward the end of June, 1784 Jefferson visited Boston and on July 1, the *Continental Journal & Weekly Advertiser* printed a description of the Virginian which included the following:

Governor Jefferson [of Virginia], who has so eminently distinguished himself in the late Glorious Revolution, is a gentleman of amiable character to which he has joined the most extensive knowledge. He is a mathematician and philosopher, as well as a civilian and politician, and the memorable Declaration of American Independence is said to have been penned by him.

Years later Jefferson, in a letter to Doctor James Mease of Philadelphia, described his surroundings as he drafted the Declaration, "At the time of writing of that instrument . . . I lodged in the house of Mr. Graff . . . of which I rented the second floor consisting of a parlor and a bedroom ready furnished. In that parlor I wrote habitually and in it wrote this paper particularly." In answer to historians who accused him of including nothing new in the document, he wrote James Madison in 1823, "I know only that I turned to neither book nor pamphlet while writing it. I did not consider it as any part of my charge to invent new ideas altogether and to offer no sentiment which had ever been expressed before."

In 1777 Jacob Graff sold his house to Jacob Hiltzheimer who rented it first to Colonel Ephraim Blaine, then to John Dunlap, publisher of the *Pennsylvania Gazette* and printer of the first copies of both the Declaration of Independence and the Constitution of the United States, and finally to James Wilson, Associate Justice of the United States Supreme Court and member of the committee which prepared the draft of the Constitution.

The daughter of Jacob Hiltzheimer, Mary Rogers, fell heir to the house on her father's death. She sold it to Simon Gratz, a prosperous merchant and leader of Philadelphia's Jewish community. For the next eighty years Gratz and his heirs used the property for a place of business. The structure was replaced in 1884 by a bank building which in turn was removed in 1933. In its place will rise the reconstructed Graff House and an adjoining interpretive center.

KOSCIUSZKO NATIONAL MEMORIAL 13

*301 Pine Street. Kosciuszko, a Polish military leader and states-
man and the first foreign officer to volunteer in the American
Revolution, lived from November, 1797, until May, 1798, in
this house which was built in 1775.*

THE shouts of the patriots in the State House Yard acclaiming the
Declaration of Independence had scarcely faded when a young Polish
military man appeared on the cobblestoned streets of Philadelphia. Thaddeus Kosciuszko, lured by romantic tales of the freedom-loving Americans,
had sailed across the Atlantic to see these people with his own eyes. The
colonists had no treasury, he had heard, and they had no army. But for
those rights that they cherished, they would go to war with the mightiest
empire in the world. The young Pole longed to cast his lot with such a
courageous underdog.

Kosciuszko had trained as a cadet in Warsaw and studied the art of
fortification in France. He knew the American military would need skills
such as his, and he volunteered his talents to the Continental Army. Thaddeus' first assignment, to fortify Philadelphia, won him the rank of Colonel
of Engineers. He designed the defenses at Saratoga, causing the victorious
General Gates to write, "The greatest tacticians of the campaign were hills
and forests which a young Polish engineer was skillful enough to select for
my encampment." His mission to secure New York from attack by way
of the Hudson River resulted in defenses constructed at West Point. Finally,
as chief engineer of the southern army, Kosciuszko took part in the siege of

Charleston and the Battle of Ninety-Six, a service that earned him a promotion to Brigadier General. When the war ended in victory for the Americans, Congress showed its gratitude by bestowing on the Polish officer the rank of Brigadier General, United States citizenship, five hundred acres of land and twelve hundred dollars.

Thaddeus Kosciuszko returned to Poland to take part in the struggles of his native land. Many strife-filled years passed, taking their toll on his health, until in 1797 his thoughts centered on man's inhumanity to man and the inevitability of death. He felt it necessary to go back once more to Philadelphia, now the capital of the United States. He had unfinished business to settle.

Many of the young patriots the Polish officer had known in the days of the Revolution had risen to high offices in government and now were sitting in Congress Hall at Sixth and Chestnut Streets. Kosciuszko was eager to renew his friendship with George Washington and to see Thomas Jefferson regarding the pension awarded him at the termination of the war.

He rented rooms in a modest brick row house in a fashionable neighborhood at Third and Pine Streets "where foreign ministers were in great numbers and all looked rich and hearty." A three-story dwelling erected just before the Revolution began, the house had two rooms on each of its three floors, a cellar-kitchen and an attic. Soon after Kosciuszko and his secretary, Julian Niemcewicz, had settled in their rooms, hospitable Philadelphians began to send invitations to Kosciuszko's door. Would he dine with them or attend evening tea parties in their drawing rooms? Or be their guest at a concert, theatre or an Assembly Ball? The ailing soldier felt well enough to dine, drink and even sing, as was the custom at tea parties, but he doubted he was up to dancing the quadrille.

Kosciuszko sent his secretary as his representative to the Dancing Assembly functions and the younger man amused him with his observations when he returned at two or three o'clock in the morning. Niemcewicz said ungallantly of Philadelphia belles:

> Two things struck me in these beauties, their big feet and their bosoms, so lean that one could scarcely consider them as such. All the women were dressed in white with silver ruffles. They appeared to like to dance; perhaps it gave them pleasure, but they took care not to show it to the onlookers. Men and women both are very far away from having that playfulness and vivacity that one sees at our balls in Warsaw . . .

His six-month stay allowed Kosciuszko more than enough time to complete his business. He collected his accumulated pension of $18,940 and entrusted it to Thomas Jefferson for investment. He instructed Jefferson that "should I die without will or testament," Jefferson was to sell the five hundred acres awarded him at the end of the war and use that money, com-

Kosciuszko House with St. Peter's church in the background.

bined with his pension, to buy Black slaves, free them and educate them. Jefferson prepared a formal will containing this provision, and it was signed by Kosciuszko on April 30, 1798.

With this Thaddeus Kosciuszko wound up his affairs in America. His spirits lifted by the vitality, integrity and nobility he saw in the nation's leaders and the "increase in all respects of the country, bespeaking future greatness," he felt strong enough physically and mentally to throw himself once again into the struggles to reform the Old World. In May he vacated the house at Third and Pine and left the United States for good.

Kosciuszko died October 15, 1817 in Switzerland, leaving two more wills which resulted in a series of court litigations lasting more than thirty years. In the end, no slaves were freed nor Blacks educated by his funds, but the gesture remains as one of the early emancipation plans devised in the United States.

Fire buckets.

TODD HOUSE

14

Fourth Street at Walnut. This house is a restoration of the building erected in 1775 in which Dolley Todd lived with her husband John and, as a young widow, entertained her suitor James Madison in 1794.

PHILADELPHIA had become the capital of the United States in 1791 when Dolley Payne Todd and her lawyer-husband bought the house at Fourth and Walnut Streets. Despite the lowing of cows in back yards and pigs grunting in the alleys, this metropolis was far from a "Greene Countrie Towne" such as William Penn envisioned in 1681. The Todds could stand at their door and over the twittering of sparrows in the poplars hear the clatter of horses' hooves and coach wheels on the cobblestoned street, scores of complaining water-pump handles being lifted and lowered, and the bell from the State House clanging the hour.

On the evening breeze blowing off the Delaware River they could sniff a potpourri of fragrances arising from bake shops, neighboring Dr. Griffitts' medicinal herb garden, blooming lilacs and roses, and the notorious stench of a nearby tannery. There was a lot to see in the nation's capital. Ladies in Paris-inspired fashions rustled along the brick pavements making their social calls, while American statesmen and foreign dignitaries with walking sticks measured their steps to City Tavern.

The Todd residence was a solidly built, three-story brick structure — the corner house of a row of attached houses erected sixteen years earlier by speculator Jonathan Dilworth. It had a connected kitchen wing with an

The Todd House.

outside rain barrel to collect water from the roof. A necessary and a stable for the horse and carriage were located in the back yard, but there was no garden. Although Philadelphia could no longer afford the space required by Penn's early city plan, "with every home pitched in the middle of its plot so that there may be grounds on each side," the property offered a "genteel and convenient home" to the young couple.

John Todd had recently been admitted to practice before the United States Supreme Court, and he and his bride of two years found it advantageous to be residing in the thick of Philadelphia notables, many of them fellow Quakers. Bishop William White lived half a block east on Walnut Street and physician Samuel Griffitts of the University Medical School lived next door. Griffitts, a Quaker, served with John on the committee of the Pennsylvania Society for the Promotion of the Abolition of Slavery. The new building of the Library Company of Philadelphia had just opened its doors two blocks away, a convenience for John Todd who belonged to the association. Most importantly, the new location offered an easily accessible lawyer's office to John's clients.

Professional men in the 1790's maintained offices in their homes. The Todds made the first-floor front room into John's law office, moving into it, among other furnishings, the lawyer's extensive collection of books, his desk and a Franklin stove. Dolley's friends often came to tea in the room to the rear of the first floor and the family dined there.

The kitchen was a bustling place run by a woman servant and a man whose job included laying the fire in each room's fireplace, caring for the horse and carriage, and scrambling to the street with leather fire buckets (kept suspended from the hall ceiling) when the frequent fire alarms sounded.

Lucy Payne, Dolley's twelve-year-old sister, occupied the upstairs rear bedroom from time to time, while the Todds slept in the master bedroom. The second-floor front room served as a parlor in which the Todds entertained guests in the evening. A law clerk named Isaac Heston and Dolley's nine-year-old brother occupied beds on the third floor.

Despite her limited schooling on a North Carolina plantation where she spent her childhood (it was thought wasteful to teach a female more than reading and writing), Dolley Payne Todd became known as an enthusiastic reader and an intelligent conversationalist. Blue-eyed, black-haired Dolley in her Quaker cap, with exquisite manners and endearing charm, would offer fruit, wine and cake to her guests and pour tea from a sterling teapot into Staffordshire china cups.

Dolley's parents, thinking people and strict Quakers, had freed their slaves and moved to Philadelphia where her father felt he could practice his religion more freely. Dolley married twenty-seven-year-old John Todd partly because he had shown great kindness to Mr. Payne in a strange city and the older man wished them to wed, but also because she found him considerate and capable of making her happy. In the house at Fourth and Walnut Streets Dolley gave birth to two sons in two years. Late in the summer of 1793 she wrote to a friend that her life held everything she had ever wanted.

But then, on the 11th of September, 1793, Thomas Jefferson dispatched a letter from Philadelphia saying, "An infectious and deadly fever has broken out in this place. Everyone is leaving the city." The most deadly epidemic of yellow fever in the history of the United States had hit the capital. Thought to have been introduced by a stricken seaman or visitor from the West Indies, the disease was spread by mosquitoes that bred in the stretches of swampland above and below densely populated Philadelphia. With no screens to keep out insects, with drinking water pumps and "necessaries" standing side by side and garbage head-high in some alleys, the yellow fever passed from one house to another and swiftly killed twenty-two percent of the city's population.

Todd House kitchen.

John Todd's law office.

On September 19, sitting at the desk in the Todd law office, Isaac Heston wrote an emotional letter to his brother:

> You cannot imagine the situation in this city. Great are the number that are called to the grave. Those who at first appeared to be stout-hearted are now moving out of the city. . . . There is now scarcely anybody to be seen . . . and those who are, are principally French and Negroes. . . . Indeed, I don't know what the people would do if it was not for the Negroes as they are the principal nurses. . . . We live in the midst of death . . . yet we have confidence and trust in our fate.

John Todd bundled Dolley and their two baby boys (the younger only six weeks old and delicate) off to the country near Gray's Ferry, hoping they would escape the disease. He, ever kind, remained in his house to minister to the legal needs of the dying.

Isaac Heston fell ill and John cared for him in the Todd house. The young clerk's condition worsened and he died. In rapid succession John's mother and then his father fell victims and passed away. Beside himself with grief and "feeling the fever" in his own veins, he hurried to Gray's Ferry to embrace Dolley just one more time before facing another day in the afflicted city. Immediately on his return, John Todd succumbed to yellow fever. It was October 24, 1793.

Dolley Todd contracted the fever and recovered, but her infant son died of it. She moved back to Philadelphia shattered by illness and sorrow. In only two weeks time she had lost her husband, son, mother- and father-in-law and countless friends and acquaintances. She was a widow, very pretty and twenty-three years old.

It was not long before the mourning widow noticed that gentlemen would station themselves where they could see her pass with her maid on the way to market. Her many admirers included James Madison, a bachelor twenty years her senior, who caught sight of her once and arranged an introduction. The future President of the United States then wooed and won Dolley in the drawing room of the Todd house.

Six months after her tragedy, Dolley Todd became Mrs. James Madison and a national figure whose popularity has never been equaled in American history. She and her son, John Payne Todd, left the Todd house forever.

In the years following 1794, various tenants occupied the Todd residence, including a widow, Mrs. Grant, and General Stephen Moylan. In 1817 Dolley deeded the property to her son who sold it to an upholsterer the next year. The upholsterer and his heirs kept the property until 1950, when they sold it to the United States government.

Restored and refurnished by Independence National Historical Park, the little house has emerged once more as an exemplary residence of Philadelphia's 1791 "Quakers of some means but moderate tastes and social life."

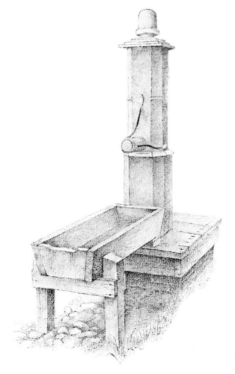

Wooden hand pump, Todd House.

BISHOP WHITE HOUSE

15

309 Walnut Street. William White, Rector of Christ Church and St. Peter's Church and the first Protestant Episcopal Bishop of Pennsylvania, built this house in 1786-87 and lived here with his family until his death in 1836.

BY 1787 Philadelphia had recovered from the commercial and industrial paralysis caused by the Revolution. Once again wheels ground over the streets of the city, bringing in lumber, iron and flour from the area west of the Schuylkill River and hauling back to Lancaster supplies for the pioneers thrusting westward.

The town William Penn had planned so meticulously one hundred years earlier to stretch from Vine to South Streets and from the Delaware to the Schuylkill rivers now had developed into a crowded triangle, the base of which followed the west bank of the Delaware while the apex was located around Tenth and Chestnut Streets.

Despite the fact that fields lay open for development beyond Tenth Street, Philadelphia builders cut alleys through the city's oldest blocks and put up rows of houses along them to accommodate a burgeoning population of about seventy thousand people, seemingly determined to dwell close to docks, markets and corner taverns.

That Philadelphia was established originally out of the "holy motivation" of William Penn, no one any longer seemed aware. Tradesmen, sailors and gentlemen alike drank excessively, while "little seamstresses" walked Market Street after dark, seducing wayward males, and thieves and debtors filled the cells of Walnut Street prison.

Into this atmosphere of wheels, hammers, shrewd dealing, vice and religious indifference stepped Bishop William White. Majestic, pink-cheeked and thirty-seven years old, he was returning to his native Philadelphia from London to revive Anglicanism in America, after having been consecrated the first Episcopal Bishop of the Protestant Church of Pennsylvania.

William's wife Mary, his children and a committee of church dignitaries greeted the tall, heron-legged figure in black silk stockings and hustled him off to see the new house his friend, Samuel Powel, had built for him in his twelve-month absence. They knew their Bishop was filled with curiosity.

For too long Bishop White had thought only of the disorganized remnant of the Episcopal Church in America. Weakened during the Revolution by inconsistent attitudes toward the British and the scattering of its clergy, Anglicanism in America had almost ceased to exist when White debarked for England. In London he had explained to the Archbishop of Canterbury that the needs of Pennsylvania (if not the nation) seemed to be: first, to recruit and train new ministers; and second, to dispel the lingering American fears of a church connected with the established Church of England.

To this end Parliament dispensed with the customary Bishop's oath of allegiance to England and the Archbishop advised White that his most important mission in his native land would be to promote harmony and make friends for his church. He seemed perfectly suited for this. Patient, wise and tactful, William differed from most clergymen of the time in that he stood ready to cooperate with men of other denominations.

Though still young, the Bishop had already served for ten years as Rector of the united congregations of St. Peter's and Christ Church in Philadelphia, a position he would hold the rest of his life. His predecessor had been the Reverend Mr. Jacob Duché, who had led the opening prayer of the First Continental Congress when it met in Carpenters' Hall in 1774, but had deserted the colonies and returned to England.

Duché's about-face left William White, at age twenty-seven, heir to St. Peter's and Christ Church's rectorships. Moreover, the Second Continental Congress swiftly nominated him their Chaplain to replace Duché, on the condition that he swear allegiance to the American cause.

It required courage for White to take that oath in 1777. Not only because American victory seemed doubtful and a hangman's noose awaited rebels, but also because such an oath made him turncoat to his British family heritage. His father, Colonel Thomas White, had emigrated from England as a youth, and William's three beloved aunts still lived there. He himself had taken Holy Orders in England, and he counted as friends many Anglican churchmen.

Still, White cast his lot on the side of independence and the culmination of the war found him Rector of the largest parish in the most centrally located and populous city in the United States and with a responsibility to rebuild the Episcopal Church in America.

Bishop White's study.

Thus, in 1787, Bishop White and his wife rattled along Water Street in their carriage, headed for Walnut Street. It was the end of the working day when sailing ships from a dozen lands lowered the last of their cargo onto the docks. Sugar and rum arrived from the West Indies, spices from Java, madeira and port wine from Portugal. Spain furnished cork, olives and olive oil, and there was coffee from Arabia, hemp from Russia, hides and ivory from Africa, and china and lacquer work from the Orient.

Traffic engulfed the carriage as sedan chairs, wagons, pushcarts, wheelbarrows and men on horseback jostled for space in the narrow streets. After weeks at sea, the cries of the drivers, snorts and whinnies of the horses and the clatter of wooden wheels on cobblestones rang painfully in the Bishop's ears. But soon his carriage turned west onto sedate Walnut Street where the din faded.

White had chosen this location for his residence because it lay halfway between the two churches he served — St. Peter's to the south and Christ Church to the north — and many of his friends lived nearby. The intelligent and witty Judge Richard Peters, secretary of the Board of War during the Revolution and founder of the Society for Promoting Agriculture, was his next-door neighbor. White's best friend, Doctor Benjamin Rush, would soon move into a house two doors away. Within a few blocks resided the most celebrated doctors and lawyers in the country, as well as most of the parishioners of his two churches.

The house on Walnut Street filled the 25- by 125-foot lot; a residence befitting a man of wealth, yet it appeared unostentatious enough for a man of cloth. The large, square rooms with twelve-foot ceilings each had fireplaces. White's friend, Samuel Powel, had made improvements in the conventional row house plan. There were three cellars below the kitchen; one for scullery and laundry, one below that for the cool storage of fruit and vegetables with the deepest level a well for the storage of ice. The "necessary" offered little seats for children and big ones for adults and instead of being located a chilling distance from the house, was attached to the rear wing beyond the kitchen. Two closets for clothes had been built into the walls of the master bedroom, and never before in America had White seen such large window panes.

Behind the house in an alley called Harmony Court stood the Bishop's new two-story stable where the coachman would live and where his horses and especially designed carriage (White measured over six feet tall) would be kept. The Bishop and his wife, their five children and three servants quickly moved into the new house.

William White had a romantic nature and he delighted in the company of young people. Music pleased him, and Mary and his two daughters played the Piano Forte in the living room to the right of the entrance hall. White opposed theatre but approved of dancing (except the waltz), and he and Mary acted as chaperones for the Dancing Assembly balls at City

Tavern. They also enjoyed entertaining. The Bishop's sister Mary and her husband Robert Morris, the financier, frequently came to dinner as did the Chews, Powels, Rushes and visiting clergy. And when Philadelphia became the capital, prominent statesmen dined with the Whites.

The Bishop worked daily in his upstairs study on correspondence. He developed his sermons and wrote *The Case of the Episcopal Church Considered,* which was a masterful analysis of church problems with suggestions for strengthening it. Acceptance of his book brought about White's elevation to Bishop of the entire Episcopal Church in the United States in 1795. The study was a place for relaxing, and White did so clad in a red coat with a white scarf. Here he smoked his two cigars a day, drank his two glasses of port and munched his daily allowance of two apples.

To cope with Philadelphia's many social problems, White organized or served on associations such as those to aid the deaf and dumb, the sick, poor, orphaned, destitute or aged, and the mistreated prisoners and prostitutes. Meetings of committees sometimes took place in his study. White formed a group to encourage Bible studies and Sunday Schools, and he founded the Episcopal Academy.

Bishop White's bed and writing desk.

Scarcely six months after moving into the Walnut Street house, the Bishop's three-year-old son Henry died. Tragedy struck again in 1797 when he lost his favorite son William, thirteen years old. And in the same year Mary, beseeching him to pray for her, passed away after two months of suffering.

The Bishop refused to give in to loneliness as the years passed and his children matured and married. He remained involved with people from every walk of life. In 1804, to his delight, his son Thomas married Maria Key Heath of Baltimore and the Bishop invited the couple to occupy his third floor so that Maria could act as his hostess. By 1826 the big house sheltered Thomas and Maria, the Bishop's daughter Elizabeth and eleven grandchildren, with the boys sleeping in the garret and girls on the third floor. The youngsters watched in awe as their eighty-five-year-old grandfather made rounds to comfort cholera victims when other men fearfully withdrew.

In 1836, still tall and straight, Bishop White was the last surviving link Philadelphia had with the giants who had declared the colonies a free and independent nation. The venerable, white-haired gentleman who "had been there" was so esteemed for his service to the people of his city that they sought his presence at every occasion from the dedication of Mikveh Israel Synagogue to a reception for Lafayette. He preached his last sermon in St. Peter's Church a few weeks before his death and passed away "sweetly and without suffering" on July 17, 1836 in his bedroom, surrounded by his son and seven of his adoring grandchildren.

The Bishop White house was sold but it remained a residence until 1858 when it became an office building. In 1951 Independence National Historical Park acquired the building and in 1960 began restoration of the gracious home as it had been when the Bishop and his family lived there.

CONGRESS HALL

16

Sixth and Chestnut Streets. Constructed 1787-89 as the Philadelphia County Courthouse, this building served as the meeting place for the United States Congress from 1790 to 1800.

I N 1732 when Andrew Hamilton offered his architectural plan for the proposed Pennsylvania State House to the Provincial Assembly, he spoke of his dream that in years to come this building would be the focal point of a government center set on a "beautiful and commodious public green."

Before Hamilton died nine years later, the Assembly put on record its intention of using the lots flanking the State House to the east and west for two buildings similar in appearance to the State House, one for the county's use, the other for the city of Philadelphia. Plans for this expansion had to be tabled, however, as problems of defense of the province and the War of Independence took precedence. It was not until 1787 that construction began on a brick County Courthouse at the southeast corner of Sixth and Chestnut Streets where a wooden lodge to house visiting Indians had stood for many years. Proceeds from the sale of Philadelphia's old jail and workhouse funded the project and, as was the custom of the day, a gang of twenty-five convicts chained to wheelbarrows dug the foundations. The courthouse stood finished in 1789.

Philadelphians, proud of their metropolis, had thought the Congress of the Confederation foolish to let the threats of a few mutinous soldiers in 1783 cause them to move from the State House to Princeton, New Jersey. Well aware of the benefits that would ensue to the city which housed the

Committee Room, Congress Hall.

new federal government, the County Commissioners offered Congress the use of the new County Courthouse. New York City countered with an offer of Federal Hall, a building which would be fully renovated by Pierre Charles L'Enfant to accommodate the august body. Such a tug of war began between the two potential host cities that newspaper editors begged those involved to stop their childishness and "let government be put in motion."

Congress agreed, but much to the dismay of Philadelphia, decided to convene in Federal Hall. Enough members had showed up in New York by March 4, 1789 to open the first session. It was not until April, however, that the votes of the presidential electors were opened, and George Washington was unanimously elected President. On April 30 he was inaugurated in one of the most spectacular ceremonies New York City has ever seen.

Then in July, 1790, near the close of the second session of the first Congress of the United States, the members approved the Residence Act which called for the building of a "Federal City" on the banks of the Potomac River and the removal to Philadelphia for a period of ten years while Washington, D.C. was being constructed. By December of that year the federal government was in residence at Philadelphia, with George Washington living near Sixth and Market Streets in a house built by Richard Penn and previously occupied in turn by General Howe, Benedict Arnold and Robert Morris. Philadelphia's mayor, aldermen and county commissioners moved out of the County Courthouse to make way for the United States House of Representatives and Senate.

Restored and decorated to receive the federal government, the structure now referred to as Congress Hall raised some eyebrows. "Too elegant," some said, "for representatives fresh from the ranks of the people." Nevertheless the Congress, with Frederick A. Muhlenberg as Speaker of the House and Vice President John Adams as leader of the Senate, settled into their respective chambers with all the assurance of Peers of England.

John Adams presided over thirty senators in a room on the second floor of Congress Hall. The senators entered the Chestnut Street door each morning, their hair white with powder, dressed in capes and suits of the richest materials. They ascended the stairs, strode down the corridor past the library and the room that adjoined the Senate Chamber where hung life-sized portraits of French King Louis XVI and Marie Antoinette, during whose reign America's treaties of alliance and commerce with France had been signed in 1778. With sedate nods to their colleagues they settled in their places. The very atmosphere of the Senate Chamber inspired "wisdom, mildness and condescension." Should a man "whisper while another was addressing the Vice President, three gentle taps with his silver pencil case by Mr. Adams immediately restored . . . the most respectful attention."

The House of Representatives Chamber on the first floor offered a remarkable contrast. Here 68 talkative representatives (106 after 1795) felt free to keep their cocked hats on their heads during sessions, to whisper to their neighbors at will, and to slouch in the two rows of mahogany chairs facing the speaker, sometimes with their feet on the desks before them.

The House had its own entrance through a small brick portico building erected in 1793 on the east side of Congress Hall. And in a niche over this entrance door stood a bust of Benjamin Franklin who had died in 1790.

The Representatives delivered "good speeches" from notes kept on the little tables before them. Frequently they drew boos or applause from an audience of some three hundred people that occupied the gallery or stood just beneath it. Foreign visitors often found the behavior of these spectators offensive, but explained their boorishness by saying, "They're full of the doctrine of equality. . . ."

In the period during which the young government sat in Congress Hall, it rectified the disordered government finances by establishing the First Bank of the United States. It refined the Legislative, Executive and Judicial branches of the federal government as well as its relationship to state governments; regulated Indian affairs; admitted the new states of Vermont, Kentucky and Tennessee to the union; ratified the Jay Treaty; established the Navy Department; and passed the Alien and Sedition acts.

On December 7, 1796 in Congress Hall, President George Washington delivered his last formal address before retiring from office. Some days later Washington's four white horses came to a halt again in front of the State House and the revered man stepped down from his coach to be cheered by a throng of admiring citizens. The crowd at Sixth and Chestnut Streets opened a path to Congress Hall for Washington to enter for the inauguration of John Adams as the second President of the United States. Three years later in this same building, grief-stricken statesmen would receive the news of George Washington's death and hear John Marshall read General Henry Lee's now famous epitaph: "First in war, first in peace, first in the hearts of his countrymen."

The federal government moved to its new quarters at Washington, D.C. in 1800, and Congress Hall once again housed the county courts and municipal departments of Philadelphia for whom it was originally intended. At the end of the nineteenth century, having long since outgrown the building, these occupants moved to a newly completed City Hall at Broad and Market Streets.

During its century of municipal service, Congress Hall had changed somewhat in appearance. The Pennsylvania Society of Colonial Dames saw the building as an important historic shrine and took action to preserve it even before the First World War. In 1913 the Philadelphia chapter of the American Institute of Architects restored it. But the final, detailed restoration of conference rooms, committee rooms, the Senate Chamber and the House of Representatives Chamber was done by Independence National Historical Park. Congress Hall looks today as it did when John Adams tapped on his desk for respectful attention.

OLD CITY HALL
(SUPREME COURT BUILDING)

17

Southwest corner of Fifth and Chestnut Streets. Constructed in 1790-91, Old City Hall served as the seat of the Supreme Court of the United States from 1791 to 1800.

WHEN the federal government moved from New York City to Philadelphia in the fall of 1790, the House of Representatives and Senate occupied the County Court House (now Congress Hall). For the Judicial branch of government, Philadelphia offered its new City Hall, a two-story brick building with a cupola just being completed on the east side of the State House.

In selecting judges for the Supreme Court, President Washington stated that he considered the system one which would "give dignity and lustre to our national character," and he named as first Chief Justice John Jay, one of the authors of the *Federalist Papers* and a man whose prestige as a lawyer and statesman exceeded even that of Madison, Hamilton and Jefferson.

A momentous task lay before the Supreme Court as it moved into a chamber designed originally as the mayor's courtroom, the large room at the south end of the first floor of City Hall. With only a few guidelines, the justices began the process that continues to this day of interpreting the precise meaning of the Constitution and the treaties and laws enacted under it. They tackled the difficult question of the Supreme Court's authority in relation to states' rights and defined the Supreme Court in relation to other branches of government. Outstanding lawyers from many states soon could be seen in the State House Yard relaxing with their colleagues during recesses, strolling the tree-shaded walks or sitting on benches among beds of shrubs and flowers studying their briefs. John Marshall and Alexander Hamilton each presented one case before the Supreme Court in this building.

City Hall, or the Supreme Court Building as it became known, measured only fifty by sixty-six feet, yet it contained six rooms used by the District and Circuit courts of the United States as well as city and state courts, the offices of the City Treasurer and City Commissioners. Often private organizations also held meetings here.

City Hall played a dramatic role in the yellow fever epidemic of 1793 that killed four thousand Philadelphians and sent twenty thousand fleeing to the countryside. At the height of the emergency the hospitals overflowed with the stricken; lifeless men, women and children lay in the streets where they fell. All business ceased and mourning bells tolled all through the day while cannon fired gunpowder to "cleanse the air of contamination." In desperation, Mayor Matthew Clarkson advertised for volunteers to meet in City Hall to help in the crisis. With twelve assistants he made City Hall the center "to avert the progress of destruction . . . relieving the distress and restoring confidence to the terrified inhabitants of Philadelphia." Again in 1797, 1798 and 1799 when yellow fever returned, City Hall made medical history by becoming the center for combating the first great epidemic in the United States.

John Jay presided as Chief Justice of the Supreme Court, sitting in City Hall until 1795. John Rutledge and Oliver Ellsworth succeeded him before the Supreme Court moved with the rest of the federal government to Washington, D.C. in 1800.

For a short time after the Supreme Court departed, lower federal courts continued to use City Hall along with the local government. At the end of the nineteenth century, agencies of the city found a new home at Broad and Market Streets in a new City Hall, and their former quarters were taken over by patriotic societies as a meeting place.

The importance of City Hall as one of the most historic structures in the United States became recognized in 1916, and six years later the city made interior alterations and opened it as a museum. Restored on the exterior by Independence National Historical Park, the building will house exhibits and displays that tell the story of the first ten years of the Supreme Court as well as of Philadelphia in the last quarter of the eighteenth century.

Old City Hall with tower of Independence Hall in the background.

Mother Bethel Church.

MOTHER BETHEL CHURCH 18

Sixth and Lombard Streets. The present structure was erected in 1890 on the site where Reverend Richard Allen and his followers formed a new denomination of the Protestant Church, known as the African Methodist Episcopal Church, and built their first house of worship in 1791.

PENNSYLVANIA outlawed slavery in 1780 and by the time Philadelphia became the temporary capital of the United States ten years later, seven thousand Black men, women and children labored there in salaried jobs ranging from sail makers to ironmongers to domestic servants.

A number of Blacks had known bondage in other states, both to the north and south, where the institution of slavery still existed. But they had managed to pay their masters in silver for their freedom and made their way to the City of Brotherly Love. Such a person was Richard Allen, a self-educated man converted to Methodism by an itinerant preacher and now himself a preacher of the gospel.

Twenty-one-year-old Allen had arrived by boat from New Castle, Delaware, as the war against England for man's right to "life, liberty and the pursuit of happiness" drew to a close. The storied city that spread before him in a blush of lamplight might have threatened another man fresh from a plantation. But Allen drew strength from the voices of his brothers bent at work all along the docks, and from the feel of the Good Book tucked in his shirt.

The young preacher found work first as a brickyard laborer, then as a chimney sweep at the State House, a job that offered more pay. He made himself known at St. George's Methodist Church at Fourth and Vine Streets where the new "sect" had been preached since just before the Revolution, and wrangled permission of its trustees to address anyone who would come to listen to him at five o'clock in the morning.

Allen soon attracted a group of Blacks to St. George's who took heart from his sermons. The preacher knew his brothers and sisters were poor and unhappy. He could see that though free, all roads upward from servitude for the unschooled Black seemed blocked by ever increasing prejudice among white workers who feared competition for their jobs. But one path still lay open to self-improvement, he told his friends: it lay in methodical study of the word of the Bible. Listen and learn in church every Sunday, he told them, and you will find a better way to live in this world and the road to glory.

Blacks began to attend the regular Sabbath service that took place at mid-morning in St. George's. Their growing number made the trustees uneasy and they announced that, in the future, Blacks would have to sit in the gallery. The Sunday after this edict Reverend Allen, his friend Reverend Absolem Jones, and several others took places in the front of the gallery overlooking their former seats, only to be told that they must move. Allen recorded the incident:

> We had not been long upon our knees before I heard . . . scuffling and low talking . . . I raised my head up and saw one of the trustees . . . having hold of the Reverend Absolem Jones pulling him off his knees and saying, "You must get up . . . you must not kneel here!" Jones requested the trustee to wait until the prayers had been completed. When he persisted and threatened force-able removal, we went out of the church in a body and they were no more plagued with us. In fact, we were filled with fresh vigor to get a house erected to worship God in.

Jones and Allen found a store they could use as a meeting house and Blacks who had walked out of St. George's Church, plus Blacks from other churches, banded into a Free African Society. They elected a committee, headed by Reverend Allen, to raise funds for a church building.

Dr. Benjamin Rush, a signer of the Declaration of Independence, contributed the most money to Richard Allen's building fund and solicited contributions from George Washington, Thomas Jefferson and Benjamin Franklin (president of the Philadelphia Society for the Abolition of Slavery). Philadelphia merchant Robert Ralston made a generous donation and agreed to serve as treasurer of the building fund, which grew despite the fact it seemed supported mostly by "swearing captains of vessels and Philadelphia brokers."

With great satisfaction Benjamin Rush attended the celebration of the roof-raising of the first church of the Free African Society in 1789 and described it in his journal: "About one hundred white . . . persons dined at one table and were waited upon by Africans. . . . Afterwards about fifty black people sat down at the same table and were waited upon by white people. ever did I see people more happy." That day Dr. Rush indulged in a favorite custom of Philadelphians: he toasted the occasion saying, "May African churches everywhere soon succeed African bondage."

The feelings of some of the members of the Free African Society still smarted from the offense they had suffered at St. George's Church. They therefore voted to affiliate themselves in a body with the Episcopal Church, not the Methodist, and they tried to persuade Richard Allen to be their pastor. Allen declined and, with some forty followers, remained faithful to Methodism for, as he later explained, "the plain and simple gospel" of Methodism best answered the spiritual needs of the Black people at the time. "All other denominations preached so high flown that we were not able to comprehend their doctrine." With Absolem Jones as their leader, part of the group then separated from Allen to form St. Thomas Protestant Episcopal Church of Philadelphia.

Two years later Allen bought a piece of ground 135 feet by 73 feet at Sixth and Lombard Streets. He paid thirty-five dollars for an old, wooden blacksmith shop, had it mounted on wheels and then hauled by ten horses to his new property. He converted this box-like structure into a meeting house, hammering together benches for his congregation and a pulpit from which he could preach. His followers soon outgrew their "church" and a bigger one became necessary.

Once again Benjamin Rush headed the subscription list for Allen's project. This time he was joined by John Nicholson and other whites who liked the preacher's plan to start a day and evening school as well as a Sunday school at the church. Construction began in the spring of 1793 and the roof-raising was celebrated on August 22 at a dinner outside of town. Little did Rush realize as he sipped apple cider with his Black friends in the shade of a giant oak tree that within three days all work on the church would stop as sultry Philadelphia gave birth to the worst yellow fever epidemic in the history of the United States.

Overnight the nation's capital turned into a fiendish place as mosquitoes carried the infection into thousands of windows along Dock Creek. Half the population fled the contagion to the clean air of Germantown and Lancaster. The hospital quickly filled and with few surviving attendants, the staff could not even separate the sick from the dead, let alone care for them.

Soon lifeless bodies littered the streets; no one dared to cart them away to the graveyards. In desperation, Mayor Matthew Clarkson ordered tar burned in the public squares to fight the disease and advertised for volunteers to help him in the emergency. Forty physicians, including Dr. Rush, remained in Philadelphia to help the stricken. To Rush's aid came

Reverend Richard Allen, Reverend Absolem Jones and a friend, William Gray. They volunteered their services without pay and recruited their friends, all of whom were still in the city as they had no country places in which to stay even if they chose to leave. A troop of Black men and women set to work under Dr. Rush's direction to cope with the crisis.

Rush instructed Allen and Jones in blood-letting and purging, the accepted treatment for yellow fever at the time. Tirelessly the two preachers moved from one house to another to offer comfort and take notes for the doctor. Then, heedless of their own safety, they helped haul away corpses by the wagon load to be buried. Not until the first frost in November did the epidemic end.

Mayor Clarkson published his thanks in the daily press of January 23, 1794 to Reverend Richard Allen, Reverend Absolem Jones and the people employed by them, "for their diligence, attention and decency."

In July Reverend Allen's church finally was finished. A large, rough-cast building some seventy feet square with a gabled roof, it fronted on Sixth Street and was surrounded by a six-foot wooden fence. The revered American Methodist Bishop, Francis Asbury delivered the dedication sermon to a proud Black congregation. Ladies were dressed in pale pink, their hair pulled back in chignons, while grandmothers in white gloves carried parasols. Men wore polished boots and carefully laundered white shirts.

Reverend John Dickins of St. George's Church followed Bishop Asbury. He read a text from the Old Testament that included the word "bethel" which, he explained, means house of God, and suggested that the congregation use this as a name for their church. The members enthusiastically approved; henceforth it would be known as the Bethel African Methodist Episcopal Church. Later, when other Bethel African churches were formed, the word "Mother" was added to distinguish it as the original.

Within a year the church, "as plain as a Quaker's coat and perfectly free from ornament," boasted a membership of about three hundred. And in 1796 the Provincial Assembly of Pennsylvania granted it a charter as an independent organization to be known as the African Methodist Episcopal Church of the City of Philadelphia and the Commonwealth of Pennsylvania. Bishop Francis Asbury ordained Reverend Richard Allen a deacon in 1799 in a service at St. George's Church, the Cradle of American Methodism. Shortly after this he officially agreed to ordain Black ministers.

In 1816 Black Methodists from various cities met in Philadelphia's Mother Bethel to establish a National Methodist Episcopal Church and elected Richard Allen, a one-time slave, the first Bishop. The Black church had become a reality in the northern United States.

A bronze plaque was unveiled in 1965 in front of the fourth structure to have been built on Richard Allen's original church site in recognition of the church's significant relationship to the historic events commemorated by Independence National Historical Park.

FIRST BANK OF THE UNITED STATES 19

120 South Third Street. Precursor of today's Federal Reserve system, the First Bank served as "banker" to the United States government and its activities regulated the nation's monetary and financial structure. The building was constructed in 1797 and housed the First Bank until 1811.

ON December 13, 1790 the first Congress of the United States, sitting in Philadelphia's Congress Hall, heard a brilliant report on government finances by Secretary of the Treasury Alexander Hamilton. The nation suffered from numerous monetary problems; most of the quarreling thirteen states had state-chartered banks and issued their own currency. Each state charged the other tariffs (Connecticut farmers, for example, had to pay a customs duty to sell their produce in New York) and the rate of exchange varied so much that a man who sailed from Georgia with fifty dollars docked in Boston to find it worth only ten. Hamilton proposed that Congress establish a national bank, modeled after the Bank of England, to bring order out of financial chaos.

The Secretary of the Treasury went on to acknowledge that Robert Morris had suggested a similar plan to the Confederation Congress in 1781 and had been authorized to establish the first true commercial bank, the Bank of North America, but had received less than satisfactory results. That facility, operating out of a store on Chestnut Street, had quickly lost its "national" character and after a few years became a local bank. The bank that Hamilton now proposed was to be different. It would serve for public

Steps of the Philadelphia Exchange with the First Bank of the United States in the background.

utility rather than private profit. It would work with the Treasury as "an indispensable engine in the administration of finances" and as the "mainspring and regulator of the whole American business world."

To the Secretary's dismay, James Madison and Secretary of State Thomas Jefferson voiced doubts as to the constitutionality of a national bank and hot opposition from a nascent Democratic-Republican Party obstructed passage of the bill for two months. Finally, on February 24, 1791, Washington signed the act to incorporate the subscribers to the Bank of the United States. The bank's charter would last twenty years. Philadelphia would become its headquarters and in a short while branch offices would be established in Boston, New York, Baltimore, Washington, Norfolk, Charleston, Savannah and New Orleans.

The bank opened for business on the second floor of Carpenters' Hall, recently vacated by the Library Company. It had an authorized capital of ten million dollars, one fifth of which was subscribed by the federal government and the balance to be sold to the public. On the morning when the bank was scheduled to open, people were lined up outside the hall. Within the first two hours, the remaining eight million dollars worth of shares were sold and the bank flourished. Well-governed by twenty-five directors who always favored "safe and prudent administration over profit-making motives," it moved into a home of its own after five years.

The new bank building faced Third Street between Chestnut and Walnut. Samuel Blodget, Jr., a versatile New England gentleman who had moved to Philadelphia when it became the nation's capital in 1790, had drawn the plans. Blodget, a sometime militia captain and successful business entrepreneur, also dabbled in architecture. He saw a unique opportunity to attempt a building in his favorite style, Renaissance Roman. He designed an elegant, polished marble front with a piazza, the top of which was supported by six fluted Corinthian columns and displayed a beautifully carved wooden pediment with an eagle standing guard over the American cornucopia of abundance.

Most Americans, never having visited the capitals of the Old World, became ecstatic over the first classic facade they had ever seen. One young lady on a sightseeing trip through Philadelphia reported to her friends that Robert Morris' new house looked like "nothing but a clump of oysters," but "'tis worth while to ride fifty miles to see the new bank . . . so very elegant, so superb I cannot give you any idea of it." And Claypoole's *American Daily Advertiser* editorialized:

As this is the first finished building of any consequence wherein true taste and knowledge have been displayed in this community, it is a pleasing task to inform its inhabitants that the architect is . . . American . . . born. . . . It may now be justly affirmed that agricultural and commercial pursuits are not the sole subjects of America's attention but that arts and sciences have already raised their infant heads with all the symptoms of beauty and wealth and vigor that promises a strong and rich maturity.

The new building with marble front and brick sides took a bite 110 feet wide by 99 feet deep out of the old Pemberton property where, before the Revolution, the walled garden with its evergreens clipped into pyramids and cones had been the scene of many genteel parties. The entire interior of the ground floor of the bank, except for the staircase area, two vault rooms and offices for the president and cashier, served as a business hall. Depositors felt secure knowing their valuables were within thick-walled vaults in the cellar, each protected by two iron-plate doors with massive rim locks.

The bank grew in power and prestige and its directors showed justifiable pride in their agency's performance which was proving to be so beneficial to the nation. Beside acting for the government and stimulating business, manufacture and commerce by providing financial facilities and capital, it exercised a wholesome influence on the rising state banks.

In 1811 the directors moved for renewal of the bank's charter, but to their dismay, the petition was denied. With attention focused on guiding the bank over the years, the directors had not foreseen that the nature of Congress, now seated in Washington, D.C., had changed and the small group originally hostile to a national bank had grown powerful enough to obstruct the charter. The Federalists had lost power and the Republicans, who denounced the bank bitterly, defeated the renewal by a close vote.

The bank closed its doors on March 3, 1811. Stephen Girard, a French immigrant who had become Philadelphia's leading merchant and who owned the largest block of shares when it ceased operations, bought the building for a bank of his own, chartered by the state. The structure on Third Street, which had been surrounded by a coachmaker's shop, a smithy and a gun factory, opened once more for business, this time as the Bank of Stephen Girard, and Girard soon became America's foremost banker.

When Girard died his bank continued operating on Third Street until 1826. Another state bank leased the old building but failed sixteen years later. Reorganized in 1847, the Girard Bank and its successor, the Girard National Bank of Philadelphia, occupied the building until 1926. After standing vacant for a few years, the American Legion used the building from 1930 to 1944. For the next twelve years it served as the principal office of the Board of City Trusts.

As part of Independence National Historical Park, the building will house exhibits and related displays that tell the story of the formation of the Executive Branch of government from 1790 to 1800, with emphasis on the Treasury Department.

SECOND BANK OF THE UNITED STATES 20

Chestnut Street between Fourth and Fifth Streets. Constructed between 1819 and 1824, his building is considered one of the finest examples of Greek Revival architecture in the United States. It housed the Second Bank until 1836 and in 1845 became the Philadelphia Customs House.

THE War of 1812, which culminated on January 8, 1815 with the defeat of the British at New Orleans, left the United States in a deplorable financial condition. The tenuous nation had almost split over the refusal in 1812 of the New England states to provide funds for the unpopular war and the question of who would pay the bills remained a strong issue after the peace. President James Madison and his followers won a difficult fight against the Federalists, led by Andrew Jackson, for a renewed national fiscal agency to solve the nation's monetary problems. On April 10, 1816 the Second Bank of the United States was chartered as a successor to the First Bank.

The new bank opened for business January 7, 1817 in temporary quarters at Carpenter's Hall and, as Madison had hoped, it soon stabilized the nation's currency and handled government funds efficiently. To establish one currency for the United States, however, the Bank refused to honor the notes issued by state and private banks and was accused of being the "instrument of a few rich and intelligent men . . . who are able to live on the labor of the many." Nevertheless, the Second Bank prospered during its first years and its directors, eyeing the activity on Chestnut Street where

Robert Morris statue and Second Bank of the United States.

fine public edifices were replacing brick houses of earlier days, soon purchased the old Isaac Norris property to provide a worthy setting for a new bank building.

An interest in Greek design had flickered in Philadelphia when the wealthiest citizens began to broaden their educations by voyaging to Europe and Athens. It occurred to the bank directors that, besides enhancing Philadelphia, a building executed in the sophisticated style of Classic Greek might show the world that appreciation of beauty as well as the pursuit of material comforts held a place in the lives of many "primitive" Americans. They announced a contest in the *Philadelphia Gazette* and other newspapers for architectural plans that would carry out an "imitation of Grecian architecture in its simplest and least expensive form." The winner of the contest was young William Strickland, and the bank building would establish his reputation as an architect.

It took five years to finish the structure on Chestnut Street, but when it was completed in 1824, it seemed a temple fit for the gods. The exterior, with porticoes on the north and the south sides, with columns of white marble "in chaste imitation of Greek architecture," had been copied from illustrations of the Parthenon in *The Antiquities of Athens* by Stuart and Revett. To the satisfaction of the architect, the directors reported shortly after moving in that Strickland's plan for the interior couldn't have been more magnificently conceived; the proportions were just right for efficiency.

Branches of the Second Bank of the United States rose in Kentucky, Indiana and New York. Each followed the lead of Philadelphia, having at least facades in the Greek style and spreading Greek Revival architecture throughout the United States.

When the Marquis de Lafayette made his sentimental return to Philadelphia in September of 1824 and passed through cheering crowds on Chestnut Street on his way to Independence Hall, veterans of the Revolutionary War, standing at attention in front of the magnificent new bank, caught his eye. The Frenchman's secretary, at a nudge from Lafayette, took note of the proud old men. But he seemed equally impressed with the building behind them, for that night he jotted in his diary, "The new bank is generally regarded as the finest specimen of architecture in the union."

During the next four years the Bank assumed national banking leadership with aristocratic Nicholas Biddle as its president and exercised a healthy influence on the financial structure of the nation. By keeping in check the lending power of the state banks, it provided a monetary system as good as any in the world and better than most.

But, "agrarian" President Andrew Jackson was determined to keep his campaign promise to the people who had supported him for election in 1828 that the bank's charter would not be renewed. His sympathies lay with the new working population of the east and the farmers and land speculators of the west who distrusted corporate banks and established "capitalists." State bank directors added their argument that Philadelphia's monied aristocracy, epitomized by Nicholas Biddle, deliberately held back the progress of other potentially great commercial centers like New York. Biddle was too conservative for the time, they complained to Jackson. Thousands of farm-born men were leaving home for the cities and creating an industrial revolution. Business in the United States must be developed on state levels by the people, not the wealthy few who held a monopoly over the nation's monetary system.

Jackson vetoed the bill to re-charter the Bank of the United States in July 1832, commenting "It is to be regretted that the rich and powerful too often bend the acts of government to their selfish purposes . . . to make the rich richer and the potent more powerful." His veto was sustained but the Bank became a central campaign issue in the election of 1832 when Conservative lawyers, merchants and intellectuals who supported Henry Clay, "leader of the aristocratic party," refused to let it die.

Jackson won by an electoral vote of 217 to 49 but Nicholas Biddle tried one last measure to wrest a new charter from Congress. He brought such pressure to bear on debtors that he was accused of deliberately attempting to start a panic. In retaliation President Jackson removed all the government's deposits from the national bank and placed them in state banks. The battle was lost. Without government deposits the Bank of the United States could continue functioning only modestly until 1836 when its charter expired. After that, it was operated as a bank under Pennsylvania state charter until 1845 when the building became the Philadelphia Customs House.

With the defeat of the Second Bank of the United States, Philadelphia lost an opportunity to become the financial capital of the United States and many years would pass before the nation's finances were truly stabilized under a workable system. In 1846 the Independent Treasury Act permitted the government to keep its money in a central treasury and in vaults located in six major cities. To facilitate mobility of credit, the first clearing house was established in New York City in 1853; Boston introduced the clearing house system in 1856 and Philadelphia two years later. A new National Banking system was inaugurated in 1863, but the monetary situation remained cumbersome until the country had suffered three major financial panics of 1873, 1893 and 1907 which led to the establishment of the present Federal Reserve Bank system in 1913.

Philadelphia's magnificent Second Bank Building was transferred from the U.S. Treasury Department to the Department of the Interior in 1939. It has been renovated and restored and now houses the portrait gallery of Independence National Historical Park. In its halls one can view the oil paintings of Charles Willson Peale and pastels of James Sharples which depict military and political personalities of the Revolutionary and early Federal eras of the country.

PHILADELPHIA EXCHANGE   21

Third and Walnut Streets. Designed by architect William Strickland and built between 1832 and 1834, it housed Philadelphia's Mercantile and Stock exchanges.

IN the first fifty years of its existence as a nation, the United States enjoyed phenomenal growth and prosperity, and Philadelphia continued to be considered ". . . superior without a doubt to every other city in the union." With sixteen hundred new buildings constructed there in the summer of 1830 alone, many people thought of Philadelphia as the "Athens of America in its public institutions, in its benevolent and charitable societies, in its literary reputation, in its site, the beautiful regularity of its streets, its buildings both public and private. . . ." But Philadelphia still lacked one facility necessary to a busy port; a mercantile building where merchants could meet to trade or sell their products.

In 1831 a society for a Philadelphia Stock Exchange was organized under five prestigious trustees, including Stephen Girard. These gentlemen, known for their decisiveness, lost no time in finding a location for the proposed exchange. They chose the fifteen-hundred-foot area bounded by Third, Walnut and Dock Streets, blighted at the time by "an uncouth mass of buildings angular, unsightly, misshapen, a proverbial deformity in our symmetrical city." The site would fit all their requirements once the objectionable structures were removed because it was close to the wharves, insurance companies, banks, the customs house and most commercial interests. The trustees hired architect William Strickland to draw plans for an exchange building at least as handsome as the Girard Bank on Third Street.

Strickland, designer of the Second Bank of the United States building as well as the United States Mint, the United States Naval Asylum in Philadelphia, the almshouse in Blockley Township and the new steeple on Independence Hall, eagerly accepted the commission. He had toured Great Britain in 1825 and had been inspired by London's Royal Exchange which boasted a new circular tower. He also had admired the circular rotunda on the exchange in New York and the exchange with a central dome in Baltimore, designed by his own teacher, Benjamin Henry Latrobe. Ever since then he had looked for an opportunity such as this to incorporate the tower and dome form into his work.

William Strickland, so enamored of Greek architecture that he repeatedly advised the pupils in his office that "the student of architecture need go no further than *The Antiquities of Athens* as a basis of design," decided to use the Choragic Monument of Lysicrates as his model for the exchange. He designed a handsome and commodious building, featuring on the interior a large exchange room with a high, domed ceiling. Rooms on the second level opened onto a gallery which looked down upon the entire exchange floor below. The building as he proposed it, with offices and meeting rooms, would draw considerable revenue.

Construction of the Philadelphia Exchange began in 1832 and the building opened for business in 1834, the architect having used only expert craftsmen who had worked for him before. From Italy he brought an outstanding painter to execute frescoes on the domed ceiling of the exchange and two stone carvers to work on the Corinthian caps, the massive stone lions and the scroll ornamentation.

The completed structure was acclaimed in the newspapers as the handsomest edifice in Philadelphia. It had marble sides measuring 114 feet, and facades, both on Dock Street to the east and Third Street to the west, ornamented with Corinthian porticoes and columns of Carrara marble. The Dock Street front, then the main entrance, had stairs on either side leading to all doors and a circular tower topped by a cupola and a weathervane.

On March 22, 1834, the Merchants' Coffee House on Second Street was badly damaged by fire and the men who for many years had been accustomed to doing business there were forced to find other quarters. Fortunately the new exchange now was completed and they transferred their affairs to it the day after the fire.

The merchants found their new accommodations at the exchange better than they had known before, as the building had been designed specifically to serve "every individual in the city and country who does anything like a wholesale business whether he be a merchant manufacturer, dry goods merchant, grocer, broker, ship master, builder, lawyer or retired capitalist." It offered a daily listing of arrivals and clearances of vessels, a bar, a reading room, a library, meeting rooms, the Philadelphia Post Office and the head-quarters of the omnibus line, which departed from the Dock Street front.

The original Exchange Company dissolved after the Civil War, and the Corn Exchange and the Philadelphia Stock Exchange took its place. Years passed and the interior of the building suffered many alterations and grew shabby. In 1922, because of the westward growth of the city, the Third Street entrance (heretofore the rear) was made the front entrance, while the more imposing Dock Street facade became the back. Eventually the edifice that had been the source of great pride to Philadelphians became a produce exchange. Its marble stairs were reduced to rubble and replaced by market sheds, while a gasoline station opened for business on its north side.

In 1952 the Philadelphia Exchange building was taken over by the National Park Service to form part of the Independence National Historical Park Project. The Park Service undertook to make the public aware of the importance of the exchange building not only as William Strickland's masterpiece, but also as one of the finest examples in the United States of the period when American architecture began to establish its own traditions.

Harmony Court behind Bishop White's house
with tower of the Philadelphia Exchange beyond.